T0085892

PRAISE FOR

The Revolt Against Humanity

"*The Revolt Against Humanity* is a profound, daring, and intellectually thrilling examination of the role of human beings on Earth: would the world be better off without us? Beautifully written, the book will spark your thoughts, challenge your preconceptions, and leave you asking yourself wonderfully unanswerable questions."

ELLEN ULLMAN,
author of *Close to the Machine* and *Life in Code*

"We're told that ideas can have momentous consequences. In that case, we owe it to ourselves to pay close attention to the chilling ideas Adam Kirsch highlights in this profound and disturbing book. On one side, some environmental activists welcome the idea that humanity may be on the brink of extinction; on the other, a group of Silicon Valley entrepreneurs dreams of using their fortunes and technical knowhow to empower us to transcend our humanity altogether. Kirsch provides an illuminating guide to both trends. He's also an uncommonly insightful critic, drawing on the wisdom of poets, novelists, and philosophers to make sense of our unsettling attraction to the idea of a world without us."

DAMON LINKER,
author of *The Theocons* and *The Religious Test*

The Revolt
Against Humanity
Imagining a Future
Without Us

COLUMBIA GLOBAL REPORTS
NEW YORK

The Revolt Against Humanity

Imagining a Future Without Us

Adam Kirsch

The Revolt Against Humanity
Imagining a Future Without Us
Copyright © 2023 by Adam Kirsch
All rights reserved

Published by Columbia Global Reports
91 Claremont Avenue, Suite 515
New York, NY 10027
globalreports.columbia.edu
facebook.com/columbiaglobalreports
@columbiaGR

Library of Congress Cataloging-in-Publication Data

Names: Kirsch, Adam, 1976- author.
Title: The revolt against humanity : imagining a future without us / Adam Kirsch.
Description: New York, NY : Columbia Global Reports, [2023] | Includes
    bibliographical references. |
Identifiers: LCCN 2022020040 (print) | LCCN 2022020041 (ebook) |
    ISBN 9781735913766 (paperback) | ISBN 9781735913773 (ebook)
Subjects: LCSH: Humanity. | Human beings. | Future, The.
Classification: LCC BJ1533.H9 K57 2023 (print) | LCC BJ1533.H9 (ebook) |
    DDC 179.7--dc23/eng/20220610
LC record available at https://lccn.loc.gov/2022020040
LC ebook record available at https://lccn.loc.gov/2022020041

Book design by Strick&Williams
Map design by Jeffrey L. Ward
Author photograph by Miranda Sita

Printed in the United States of America

CONTENTS

9
Introduction

14
Chapter One
How Could We Drink Up the Sea?

25
Chapter Two
Now It's Too Late to Change

37
Chapter Three
Humans Are Not the Point

52
Chapter Four
Fashion Yourself in the Form You May Prefer

66
Chapter Five
A Throwing Away of All the Human Rules

84
Chapter Six
The Sphere of Spiritual Warfare

99
Further Reading

Introduction

"Man is an invention of recent date. And one perhaps nearing its end." With this declaration in *The Order of Things* (1966), French philosopher Michel Foucault heralded a new way of thinking that would transform the humanities and social sciences. Foucault's central idea was that the ways we understand ourselves as human beings aren't timeless or natural, no matter how much we take them for granted. Rather, the modern concept of "man" was invented in the eighteenth century, with the emergence of new ways of thinking about biology, society, and language, and eventually it will be replaced in turn.

As Foucault writes in the book's famous last sentence, one day "man would be erased, like a face drawn in the sand at the edge of the sea." It's an eerie image, but he claimed to find it "a source of profound relief," since it implies that human ideas and institutions aren't fixed once and for all. They can be endlessly reconfigured, maybe even for the better. This was the liberating promise of postmodernism: the face in the sand is swept away,

10   but someone will always come along to draw a new picture in a different style.

But the image of humanity can only be redrawn so long as there are human beings to do it. Even the most radical twentieth-century thinkers stop short at the prospect of the actual extinction of the species *Homo sapiens*, which would mean the end of all our projects, values, and meanings. Humanity may be destined to disappear someday, but almost everyone would agree that the day should be postponed as long as possible, just as individuals generally try to delay the inevitable end of their own lives.

In recent years, however, a disparate group of thinkers has begun to challenge this core assumption. From Silicon Valley boardrooms to rural communes to academic philosophy departments, a seemingly inconceivable idea is being seriously discussed: that the end of humanity's reign on Earth is imminent, and that we should welcome it. The revolt against humanity is still new enough to appear outlandish, but it has already spread beyond the fringes of the intellectual world, and in the coming years and decades it has the potential to transform politics and society in profound ways.

This book aims to provide an introduction to the key ideas and thinkers shaping the new worldview, to understand its historical background and the sources of its appeal, and to think about its possible implications for the future. What I am calling the revolt against humanity finds support among very different kinds of people: engineers and philosophers, political activists and would-be hermits, novelists and paleontologists. Not only do they not see themselves as a single movement, but in many cases they would want nothing to do with one another. Indeed, I will try to show that the turn against human primacy is being driven by two ways of thinking that appear to be opposites.

The first is Anthropocene antihumanism, inspired by revulsion at humanity's destruction of the natural environment. The idea that we are out of tune with nature isn't new; it has been a staple of social critique since the Industrial Revolution. Half a century ago, Rachel Carson's *Silent Spring,* an exposé of the dangers of DDT, helped inspire modern environmentalism with its warning about following "the impetuous and heedless pace of man rather than the deliberate pace of nature." But environmentalism is a meliorist movement, aimed at ensuring the long-term well-being of humanity, along with other forms of life. Carson didn't challenge the right of humans to use pesticides; she simply argued that "the methods employed must be such that they do not destroy us along with the insects."

In the twenty-first century, Anthropocene antihumanism offers a much more radical response to a much deeper ecological crisis. It says that our self-destruction is now inevitable, and what's more significant, that we should welcome it as a sentence we have justly passed on ourselves. Some antihumanist thinkers look forward to the actual extinction of our species, while others predict that even if some people survive the coming environmental apocalypse, civilization as a whole is doomed. Like all truly radical movements, Anthropocene antihumanism begins not with a political program but with a philosophical idea. It is a rejection of humanity's traditional role as Earth's protagonist, the most important being in creation.

Transhumanism, by contrast, glorifies some of the very things that antihumanism decries—scientific and technological

12 progress, the supremacy of reason. But it believes that the only
way forward for humanity is to create new forms of intelligent
life that will no longer be *Homo sapiens*. Some transhumanists believe that genetic engineering and nanotechnology will
allow us to alter our brains and bodies so profoundly that we
will escape human limitations like mortality and embodiment.
Others look forward, with hope or trepidation, to the invention
of artificial intelligences infinitely superior to our own. These
beings will demote humanity to the rank we assign to animals—
unless they decide that their goals are better served by wiping
us out completely.

The antihumanist future and the transhumanist future are
opposites in most ways, except the most fundamental: they are
worlds from which we have disappeared, and rightfully so. The
attempt to imagine and embrace a world without us is the thread
that connects the figures discussed in this book. In exploring
these visions of a humanless world, I will not try to evaluate the
likelihood of their coming true. I recognize that some of the predictions and exhortations we will encounter are so extreme that
it is tempting not to take them seriously, if only as a defense
mechanism.

But the premise of the book is that the revolt against
humanity is a real and significant phenomenon even if it is "just"
an idea, and its predictions of a future without us never come
true. After all, disappointed prophecies have been responsible
for some of the most important movements in history, from
Christianity to Communism. The revolt against humanity isn't
yet a movement on that scale, and might never be, but I believe it
belongs in the same category. It is a spiritual development of the

first order, a new way of making sense of the nature and purpose
of human existence.

To understand the revolt against humanity in these terms is to see it as more than a response to the ecological and technological crises of the last ten or twenty years. Rather, those crises—from climate change to the rise of artificial intelligence—have prompted a new approach to problems that have been at the center of modern thought since Darwin and Nietzsche in the nineteenth century. To understand Anthropocene antihumanism and transhumanism, it's necessary to listen not only to tech entrepreneurs and environmental activists, but to poets, novelists, and philosophers, who often serve as a better seismograph for the future.

It's because the revolt against humanity speaks to such deep needs that it has the potential to transform the "real world" of politics and society, culture and business, in ways that I explore in the last chapter. These scenarios are necessarily speculative, and the notion that human beings could turn against humanity and embrace their own elimination might sound unbelievable. But if the twenty-first century has taught us anything so far, it's that ideas that once seemed unserious and out-of-bounds have the power to change the world.

How Could We Drink Up the Sea?

In the 2006 film *Children of Men*, director Alfonso Cuarón takes just a few moments to establish a world without a future. The movie opens in a London café in 2027, where a TV news report announces that the youngest person on Earth has just been killed in Buenos Aires; he was eighteen years old. Since 2009, in other words, humans have mysteriously lost the ability to bear children, and the film depicts a society breaking down in the face of imminent extinction. Moments after the news report, the café is blown up by a terrorist bomb.

The extinction scenario in the film, loosely based on a novel by the English mystery writer P. D. James, remains in the realm of science fiction—for now. But in October 2019, London actually did erupt in civil disorder when activists associated with the group Extinction Rebellion, or XR, blocked commuter trains at rush hour. At one underground station, a protester was dragged from the roof of a train and beaten by a mob. In the following months, XR members staged smaller disruptions at the

International Criminal Court in The Hague, New York's Wall
Street, and the South Australian state parliament.

The group is nonviolent on principle, but it embraces
aggressive tactics like die-ins and mass arrests to shock the
public into recognizing that the end of the human species isn't
just the stuff of movie nightmares. It is an imminent threat
arising from anthropogenic climate change, which threatens
to render large parts of the globe uninhabitable. Roger Hallam,
one of the founders of XR, has described the coming ecological
catastrophe as a second, deadlier Holocaust: "The Nazi Holocaust that led to all of Europe saying 'never again.' But it is happening again, on a far greater scale and in plain sight." To avert
this fate, XR calls for reducing greenhouse gas emissions to net
zero by 2025, a goal that would require immediate deindustrial-
ization around the world. The pain involved in such a step is justified because the lives of billions hang in the balance.

Since 2006, when Al Gore's documentary *An Inconvenient
Truth* brought the evidence of man-made climate change to a
wide audience, the idea that the planet is on course for environmental catastrophe has become increasingly mainstream.
Hallam, of course, is a radical. In his pamphlet *Common Sense
for the 21st Century* (2019), an updating of Thomas Paine for
the age of climate change, he calls for the government of the
UK to be replaced by a National Citizens' Assembly, chosen
by lot and tasked with remaking society to address the climate
crisis.

But Hallam's use of terms like "extinction" and "genocide"
is far from unusual in today's environmental discourse. Jour-
nalist David Wallace-Wells rendered the same verdict in *The*

16   *Uninhabitable Earth* (2019), marshaling evidence for the idea that climate change "is not just the biggest threat human life on the planet has ever faced but a threat of an entirely different category and scale. That is, the scale of human life itself." The book catalogues the likely effects if Earth's atmosphere continues to get warmer due to the emission of carbon dioxide from burning fossil fuels: flooding of coastal cities as the sea level rises, refugee crises, and wars as hundreds of millions of people flee equatorial zones, mass death from heat exposure, and crop failure.

Wallace-Wells notes that it's hard to write about such a future without sounding like a religious prophet, using "perennial eschatological imagery inherited from existing apocalyptic texts like the Book of Revelation." The resemblance is heightened by the way climate-change discourse has gravitated toward an actual date for the end of the world. According to a 2018 report by the UN's Intergovernmental Panel on Climate Change, limiting the rise in global average temperatures to 1.5 degrees Celsius would require a 45 percent decrease in carbon dioxide emissions by 2030. This was widely reported as meaning that the planet "has only until 2030 to stem catastrophic climate change," in the words of one CNN headline.

Scientists have warned that it is incorrect and counterproductive to suggest that the climate problem has a fixed deadline. But with 2030 given such outsize importance, it's no wonder that, as Rep. Alexandria Ocasio-Cortez remarked in 2019, "Millennials and Gen Z and all these folks that come after us" believe that "the world is going to end in twelve years if we don't address climate change." Indeed, according to a 2020 poll by the American Psychiatric Association, 55 percent of those surveyed were "somewhat or extremely anxious" about the impact of climate change on their own mental health, with the figure rising to 67 percent for people aged eighteen to twenty-three. Greta Thunberg, the young climate activist from Sweden, channeled that generational anxiety in a series of speeches, declaring at the UN's Climate Action Summit in 2019: "People are suffering. People are dying. Entire ecosystems are collapsing. We are in the beginning of a mass extinction."

The idea that the world is heading for a mass extinction event, comparable to those that altered the course of evolution in the remote past, was introduced to a wide public by Elizabeth Kolbert's Pulitzer Prize—winning book, *The Sixth Extinction* (2014). In telling the story of five earlier extinctions—such as Cretaceous-Tertiary extinction 66 million years ago, in which an asteroid strike destroyed the majority of life on Earth—Kolbert emphasizes the fragility of our ecosystem, the way it depends on a precise balance that can be suddenly upset. "What this history reveals, in its ups and its downs, is that life is extremely resilient but not infinitely so," she writes. "There have been very long uneventful stretches and very, very occasionally 'revolutions on the surface of the earth.'"

Kolbert argues that we are in the midst of one of those revolutions, in which "one-third of all reef-building corals, a third of all freshwater mollusks, a third of sharks and rays, a quarter of all mammals, a fifth of all reptiles, and a sixth of all birds are headed toward oblivion." This mass extinction is unique because it's the first to be caused not by cosmic or geological forces, but by human activity. As Kolbert writes, "Those of us alive today not only are witnessing one of the rarest events in life's history, we are also causing it."

18   The Sixth Extinction doesn't necessarily entail that humans will be among the species to go extinct. But the prospect of billions of human deaths naturally concentrates the mind on our environmental future better than stories about the disappearance of other species like tree frogs, and many climate activists treat mass death as a certainty—"not a matter of ideology, but of simple maths and physics," Hallam writes.

The idea that life on Earth faces imminent catastrophe due to human recklessness is not entirely new. Since the late 1940s, humanity has lived with the knowledge that it has the power to annihilate itself at any moment through nuclear war. Indeed, the climate anxiety of the 2010s can be seen as a return of apocalyptic fears that went briefly into abeyance after the end of the Cold War. Climate activism features some of the same tropes as nuclear activism: sixteen-year-old Greta Thunberg urging the US Congress to avert climate disaster was reminiscent of ten-year-old Samantha Smith, who in 1982 wrote a widely publicized letter to Soviet premier Yuri Andropov asking him to avert nuclear war.

But the idea that humanity will destroy itself through environmental despoliation has more profound repercussions than the idea that it might destroy itself through an act of war. Nuclear war is the ultimate evil, but the belief that war is evil is nothing new. By raising the stakes of war, nuclear weapons give new cogency to the critique of violence that lies deep in all moral and religious traditions. To avoid nuclear annihilation means practicing values of peace and cooperation that we already preach.

The idea that we will destroy ourselves by despoiling the planet is more radically unsettling. It means that humanity is

endangered not only by our acknowledged vices, such as hatred
and violence, but by pursuing aims that we ordinarily consider
good and natural: prosperity, comfort, increase of our kind. The
Bible gives the negative commandment "thou shalt not kill" as
well as the positive commandment "be fruitful and multiply,"
and traditionally they have gone together. But if being fruitful
and multiplying starts to be seen as itself a form of killing, since
it deprives future generations and other species of irreplace-
able resources, then the flourishing of humanity can no longer
be seen as simply good.

Instead, it becomes part of a zero-sum competition that
pits the gratification of human desires against the well-being
of all of nature—not just animals and plants, but soil, stones,
and water. If that's the case, then humanity can no longer be
considered a part of creation or nature, as science and religion teach in their different ways. Instead, it must be seen as an
anti-natural force that has usurped and abolished nature, sub-
stituting its own will for the processes that once appeared to be
the immutable basis of life on Earth.

This understanding of humanity's place outside and against
the natural order is summed up in the term "Anthropocene,"
which in the last decade has become one of the most important
concepts in the humanities and social sciences. Technically
speaking, the Anthropocene is a proposed designation for a new
geological era to follow the Holocene, the era that began about
11,000 years ago with the end of the last ice age. The International Commission on Stratigraphy, the scientific body that
formally determines the names and dates of geological epochs,
has been considering since 2008 whether to determine that we
have now entered the Anthropocene or "human era" instead.

20   Whatever the ICS decides, however, the Anthropocene has already left its origins in geology far behind. As environmental scientist Erle C. Ellis has written, "The significance of the Anthropocene resides in its role as a new lens through which age-old narratives and philosophical questions are being revisited and rewritten," especially the "narrative relating humans and nature." In particular, it breaks with a central principle of scientific thought since Darwin—the naturalization of humanity, the insistence that humans can only be understood as a part of the same evolutionary process that created every other form of life.

As Ellis writes, "For most natural scientists, humans have long been a sideshow; the main stage occupied by the natural world and its processes, from physics to chemistry to biology. Compared with these 'great forces of nature' and their billions of years of unbroken history, we humans are just another animal— and a newcomer at that." The Anthropocene doesn't deny that human beings are the product of natural forces, but it puts an end to the notion that this is a one-way process. The nature that produced humanity is now itself produced by humanity.

Legal scholar Jedediah Purdy offers a good definition of this paradigm shift in his book *After Nature* (2015): "The Anthropocene finds its most radical expression in our acknowledgment that the familiar divide between people and the natural world is no longer useful or accurate. Because we shape everything, from the upper atmosphere to the deep seas, there is no more nature that stands apart from human beings." We find our fingerprints even in places that might seem utterly inaccessible to human beings—in the accumulation of plastic on the ocean floor and the thinning of the ozone layer six miles above our heads.

Humanity's domination of the planet is so extensive that evolution must be redefined. The survival of the fittest, the basic mechanism of natural selection, now means the survival of what is most useful to human beings. The Anthropocene has been catastrophic for tree frogs, but it is a boon for animals we like to eat: "Domesticated chickens are now Earth's most abundant bird and cattle biomass alone exceeds that of all other living vertebrate animals combined—including humans," Ellis writes.

In the Anthropocene, nature becomes a reflection of humanity for the first time. The effect is catastrophic, not only in practical terms, but spiritually. Nature has long filled for secular humanity one of the roles once played by God, as a source of radical otherness that can humble us and lift us out of ourselves. In the eighteenth century, Edmund Burke characterized this experience as "the sublime," and observed that it is uniquely associated with nature, while "the beautiful" is produced by artifice.

Burke argues that this is because sublimity involves feelings of astonishment and fear, which can only be produced by confronting forces incomparably greater and more powerful than ourselves. "Terror is . . . the ruling principle of the sublime," he writes, giving the ocean as an example: "A level plain of a vast extent on land is certainly no mean idea; the prospect of such a plain may be as extensive as a prospect of the ocean; but can it ever fill the mind with anything so great as the ocean itself? This is owing to several causes; but it is owing to none more than this, that the ocean is an object of no small terror."

22   The sublime isn't only for aesthetes and landscape painters. Some of its greatest appreciators have been scientists, who are uniquely qualified to appreciate the power and scale of nature. In *The Voyage of the Beagle*, Darwin writes of the "sublimity" he found in South America's "primeval forests undefaced by the hand of man": "No one can stand in these solitudes unmoved, and not feel that there is more in man than the mere breath of his body."

Today, these grand works of nature no longer evoke awe but its direct opposite, pity. In the Anthropocene, we understand oceans, forests, and glaciers as being endangered by us, not the other way around. One of the symbols of our age is the Great Pacific Garbage Patch, a swirling mass of waste halfway between California and Hawaii that is three times the size of France. How can we escape from ourselves by contemplating a world we have so comprehensively defaced?

One of the first observers to understand the significance of this change was writer and activist Bill McKibben. In *The End of Nature* (1989), a landmark work of environmentalist thought, McKibben warned of the melting glaciers and superstorms that are now our everyday reality. But the real subject of the book was our traditional understanding of nature as a "world entirely independent of us which was here before we arrived and which encircled and supported our human society." This idea, McKibben wrote, was about to go extinct, "just like an animal or a plant"—or like Foucault's "man," erased by the tides. Animals and plants, ocean and weather, will of course continue to exist, but they will no longer provide "the retreat from the human world, the sense of permanence, and even of eternity" that we used to find in nature. "We have killed off nature," McKibben

declared, a decade before the term "Anthropocene" was coined
as an epitaph.

Deliberately or not, McKibben's language echoed the
famous parable of the madman in which Friedrich Nietzsche
announced the death of God a century earlier. For Nietzsche,
too, the crucial fact wasn't only that God was dead, but that he
died at human hands: "We have killed him—you and I. All of us
are his murderers. But how did we do this? How could we drink
up the sea?"

The ocean metaphor is telling: only in nature can we find
realities vast and mighty enough to serve as symbols of the
divine. Now, in the Anthropocene, we have done to the reality
of nature what we once did to the idea of God. By killing God,
Nietzsche suggests, humanity revealed to itself that God was
never anything more than an idea of its own creation—which
means that humanity was more powerful than God all along.
This revelation of our own power is the most deranging consequence of the death of God. As the madman demands, "Is
not the greatness of this deed too great for us? Must we ourselves not become gods simply to appear worthy of it?" This
challenge is the basis of Nietzsche's concept of the superman,
the fearless being "beyond good and evil" that we must strive
to become.

In our time, the Anthropocene poses an equally profound challenge. If the killing of God demands the birth of the
superman, the killing of nature demands the creation of the
posthuman—a new being equal to the task of ruling a denat-
uralized world. The idea of the posthuman gives rise to aspirations that are both ideological—a new way of thinking about
what we are—and technological—an actual transformation of

24   the world and of our own bodies. For the same technological power that enables us to remold nature also makes it possible to remake ourselves, in ways that used to seem equally unthinkable. Once we have done away with nature as a limiting concept, why should human nature be an exception?

Now It's Too Late to Change

For mainstream environmentalists, solving the climate crisis is a matter of enlightened self-interest. We are faced with a species-level marshmallow test: if we burn all our fuel and cut down all our forests today, there will be nothing left for tomorrow. One strategy has been to establish easily understood numerical targets for limiting the damage. The 2015 Paris Agreement commits the 196 signatory nations to "holding the increase in the global average temperature to well below 2°C above pre-industrial levels and pursuing efforts to limit the temperature increase to 1.5°C above pre-industrial levels." The group 350.org, founded by Bill McKibben in 2007, takes its name from the goal of limiting CO_2 in the atmosphere to 350 parts per million.

But even the advocates of these goals acknowledge that they are very unlikely to be met. The Paris targets are nonbinding, with no mechanism for enforcement, and according to NOAA, in 2019 the global average CO_2 level was already 410 ppm. The evident failure of our political and economic systems to achieve

26   sustainability creates an opportunity for advocates of more radical change. Naomi Klein, long a leading critic of neoliberalism
and globalization, began to harness those themes to environmentalism in her 2014 book, *This Changes Everything: Capitalism
vs. the Climate.* "Climate change," Klein writes, "could become a
galvanizing force for humanity, leaving us all not just safer from
extreme weather, but with societies that are safer and fairer in
all kinds of other ways as well."

Klein argues that environmental degradation and economic inequality are symmetrical problems, both caused by the
exploitative greed of the rich and the governments and corporations they control. "Our problem has a lot less to do with the
mechanics of solar power than the politics of human power—
specifically whether there can be a shift in who wields it, a shift
away from corporations and toward communities," Klein writes.
In *After Nature*, Purdy makes a similar left-liberal argument that
the solution to environmental crisis lies in a more egalitarian
society. "The Anthropocene question—what kind of world to
make together—should be taken as a challenge to democracy,"
he writes.

To a greater degree than Klein, however, Purdy recognizes
that preserving the environment poses a challenge democracies
are ill-equipped to address, because it requires a commitment
to "self-restraint." Instead of achieving equitable economic
growth—a problem that already seems to defy democratic solution in America—a democracy for the Anthropocene would
have to renounce growth altogether. As Purdy writes, "The ultimate political challenge is to limit, together and legitimately,
the scope of human appetites, so that we do not exhaust and
undo the living world."

The problem of limit isn't just about economics. Fundamentally, it is about whether human beings can ever voluntarily relinquish control over our world. For it is only when we set limits to our own power that nature can achieve, in Purdy's words, "some definite shape, some stability in its climate and seasons, some diversity in species and habitats and landscapes." Kabbalah, the tradition of Jewish mysticism, says that to create the world God underwent *tzimtzum,* a process of voluntary contraction, in order to leave an open space for the cosmos to exist in. Now that humanity has godlike power over the earth, we must do the same if we want to preserve it.

It's difficult to get people to give up bad habits on the basis of a long-term cost-benefit analysis; otherwise, all smokers would quit immediately. But it can be easier when the giving-up is understood as serving a higher purpose—that is, as a sacrifice. People regularly renounce certain foods or sex, mortify their bodies, or march to death on the battlefield as a sacrifice to God or country. Some of the best environmentalist writing attempts to cultivate a similar mystique around the idea of nature, in order to encourage sacrifices on its behalf.

Biologist E. O. Wilson named this mystique or affect "biophilia," a fascination with living creatures simply because they are alive. "The living world is the natural domain of the most restless and paradoxical part of the human spirit," he writes in his classic book *Biophilia* (1984). "Our sense of wonder grows exponentially: the greater the knowledge, the deeper the mystery and the more we seek knowledge to create new mystery." This formula suggests how the environmentalist mystique of nature differs from the animism and nature-worship of the pre-scientific past. In myth, nature is revered because it is

28   incomprehensible, the domain of gods and chthonic powers. For Wilson and other scientific environmentalists, nature deserves reverence for the opposite reason—because it is amazingly comprehensible, with so many secrets to unlock. Even dirt partakes of this mysterious knowability, Wilson writes: "This unprepossessing lump contains more order and richness of structure, and particularity of history, than the entire surfaces of all the other (lifeless) planets. It is a miniature wilderness that can take almost forever to explore."

The problem is that the human desire to know isn't pure. We pursue understanding primarily in order to achieve mastery, to change the earth into forms more suitable to our desires. "We are killing the thing we love, our Eden, progenitrix, and sibyl," Wilson wrote in *Biophilia*. Three decades later, in *Half-Earth* (2016), he argued that since humanity has failed to moderate its environmental impact, the time has come to perform a literal act of *tzimtzum* and contract our presence to just half of the planet's surface. He outlines a plan for building on existing national parks and nature preserves to protect the other half, including the most unique and endangered habitats. This would allow much of Earth's biosphere to recover from the damage we've inflicted; Wilson estimates that removing ourselves from 50 percent of the planet would save 85 percent of its species.

Yet even this dramatic embrace of limit can be seen as a product of Anthropocene thinking, rather than a cure for it. While Wilson denies that human beings have infinite power over nature—"We are not as gods. We're not yet sentient or intelligent enough to be much of anything," he scoffs—the half-Earth idea implicitly confirms that nature is ours to shape as we will. Whether we decide to exploit the entire planet or withdraw from half of it, the fate of the earth depends on human decisions.

What's more, to support Earth's entire population using half of the available resources will require the development of new technologies, accelerating humanity's trajectory away from nature. "Food production per hectare sharply raised by indoor vertical gardens with LED lighting, genetically engineered crops and microorganisms," and other such technologies will "yield more and better results with less per-capita material and energy, and thereby will reduce the size of the ecological footprint," Wilson writes. In other words, as half the earth returns to Eden, the other half will be moving more rapidly into the Anthropocene. Wilson's version may use less fossil fuels, but it encloses humanity even more securely in a world of its own devising.

This is the trap in which human-centered environmentalism sooner or later finds itself. We may restrain our activity in the hope of leaving more room on the planet for nonhuman life to flourish. But as long as there are seven billion—plus human beings to feed and shelter, to keep warm, clothed, and comfortable, it is simply impossible to climb down from the teetering height of twenty-first-century technology. We have to keep pushing further into the Anthropocene, in the hope that we will somehow come out the other end into a green world.

In short, as English writer Paul Kingsnorth complains in his 2011 essay "Confessions of a Recovering Environmentalist," "Today's environmentalism is about people." Kingsnorth is one of the most interesting and significant thinkers about the

30   Anthropocene because he reverses the usual terms of the discussion. Instead of thinking of the environment as the problem, he thinks of the existence of human beings as the problem.

It is because he took this step that Kingsnorth, a veteran English campaigner for green and anti-globalization causes, no longer thinks of himself as an environmentalist. He writes that he came to understand environmentalism as simply another component of the industrial civilization it claims to fight, "the catalytic converter on the silver SUV of the global economy." To reduce fossil fuel consumption, for instance, green energy advocates look to renewable sources like wind. But "stand on the dunes at Walney Island" off the west coast of England, Kingsnorth writes, "and look out to sea, and the horizon is filled by wind turbines bigger, and in greater number, than you thought wind turbines could ever be. Never mind the cozy green fantasies about 'human-scale' renewable energy: this is the future and, like the past, it is breathtakingly vast in its ambition and its engineering."

To make Wilson's vision of half-Earth a reality, much of the inhabited half would have to be similarly transformed. That's fine if one's objection to the Anthropocene is pragmatic, a matter of safeguarding ourselves against ecological crisis. But it does nothing to resolve the metaphysical crisis of the abolition of nature. A will that chooses to limit itself to half the planet is still sovereign over the whole.

If the only way to restore the sovereignty of nature is for human civilization to collapse, then Kingsnorth welcomes the prospect. In 2009, he and coauthor Dougald Hine published *Uncivilization: The Dark Mountain Manifesto*, in which they seceded from the basic premise of mainstream environmentalism: "We do not believe that everything will be fine. We are not even sure, based on current definitions of progress and improvement, that we want it to be." Kingsnorth longs not for progress but for a return to the unpopulated landscapes he knew as a child: "the relief of escaping from the towns and the villages, away from the pylons and the pubs and the people, up onto the moors again, where only the ghosts and the saucer-eyed dogs and the old legends and the wind can possess me."

If he must choose between nature and humanity, Kingsnorth chooses the former, with full awareness of where such a decision may lead. In the celebrated essay "Dark Ecology," he writes about his uncomfortable realization that his views resembled those of Ted Kaczynski, the Unabomber, who believed that "only the collapse of modern technological civilization can avert disaster." Kingsnorth rejects terroristic violence, advocating instead for individual withdrawal from the system: "Withdraw because action is not always more effective than inaction," he urges. But he recognizes that even nonviolent varieties of Anthropocene antihumanism involve an adverse judgment on the human species. Antihumanists reject any claim humanity might once have had to admiration and solidarity. Instead, they invest their admiration in the nonhuman: animals, plants, rocks, water, air. Any of these entities is superior to humanity, for the simple reason that it doesn't destroy all the others.

There are precedents for this denigration of the human. Since the Industrial Revolution, poets have often brought humanity before the bar of nature and found it wanting. Wordsworth complained, "Little we see in Nature that is ours; / We have given our hearts away, a sordid boon!" Whitman declared, "I think I could turn and live with animals, they are so placid and

32   self-contained. . . . Not one is dissatisfied, not one is demented with mania of owning things."

But the poet who most nearly predicts Anthropocene antihumanism is Robinson Jeffers, a twentieth-century American writer who described his philosophy as "inhumanism." For Jeffers, who spent much of his life in remote Carmel, California, humanity was a contamination on an otherwise beautiful planet. In his poem "The Place for No Story," he describes an austere landscape on the California coast—rock, ocean, hawks—and concludes: "This place is the noblest thing I have ever seen. No imaginable / Human presence here could do anything / But dilute the lonely self-watchful passion."

Jeffers demonstrates the tendency of antihumanism to turn into misanthropy. Kingsnorth's Dark Mountain movement takes its name from Jeffers's poem "Rearmament," written in 1935 as World War II approached. For the poet, "these grand and fatal movements toward death" looked like condign punishment:

> The beauty of modern
> Man is not in the persons but in the
> Disastrous rhythm, the heavy and mobile masses, the
>   dance of the
> Dream-led masses down the dark mountain.

In our time, humanity is sleepwalking down the dark mountain of the Anthropocene to an even more comprehensive doom. How could the few who are awake to the danger fail to despise the many who are "dream-led"? One reason for Greta Thunberg's popularity is that, as a teenager, she had special

permission to express this punitive anger, which more established figures tend to avoid as undignified or counterproductive. "I don't want you to be hopeful. I want you to panic. I want
you to feel the fear I feel every day," Thunberg told the World
Economic Forum in Davos in 2019.

Thunberg's speeches are calls to action, which implies that
there are remedial actions to take and that people are capable of
taking them. But for the most committed antihumanists of the
Anthropocene, the corruption of our species goes deeper than
today's feckless governments and corporations. The state of the
planet reveals that humanity is essentially a destroyer, and has
been from the very beginning of its appearance on the planet.

This idea doesn't only appeal to poets and hermits. British
paleobiologist Michael Boulter advances it with scientific rigor
in *Extinction: Evolution and the End of Man* (2002), a survey of
humanity's ecological impact since the Stone Age. Before
human beings arrived in Scotland about 4,000 years ago,
Boulter writes, "mammals, birds, and other animals were inte-
grated to form a stable balanced ecosystem. There was no waste.
As in all natural systems, the ecosystem was built and controlled
from within. It had a kind of peace and harmony."

Humans didn't need bulldozers to destroy this demi-
Paradise; the technologies of 2100 BC, such as fire and herding,
were enough to shatter it beyond repair. "For the first time,"
Boulter writes, "a species interfered consciously with the balance of nature, taking things from it, changing it for its own
advantage." In fact, by then humanity's record was already
bloodstained. Paleontology suggests that humans hunted many
large mammals to extinction in Europe—including the mam-
moth, woolly rhino, elk, hyena, lion, bear, and tiger—about

34   21,000 years ago. The ancestors of the Native Americans walked across what is now the Bering Strait about 11,000 years ago, and "within a few thousand years of their migration 70 percent of the species of large mammals in North America were extinct," Boulter writes.

Many of those large mammals were predators themselves, and all species "take things" from nature for their own advantage. But for Boulter, human predation is in a different class morally, since only we are clever and insatiable enough to destroy whole ecosystems. Once we understand this, our final judgment on our species must be negative. "We have grown up to give reverence to the advanced characters of *Homo sapiens*, and now we know they were flawed," Boulter writes. There's no reason to believe that a species that has displayed "aggressive selfishness" from the very beginning will be able to call a halt to its exploitation, even when its own survival is threatened, Boulter concludes: "Now it's too late to change and we cannot organize ourselves to stop."

Roy Scranton is a writer and Iraq War veteran, not a scientist like Boulter, but in *Learning to Die in the Anthropocene* (2015) he comes to the same conclusion just by looking at the contemporary world, from burning oil refineries outside Baghdad to Hurricane Katrina. "We're fucked. The only questions are how soon and how badly," he writes. The collapse of human civilization will cause great suffering, but Scranton finds it impossible to regret, since "carbon-fueled capitalism is a zombie system, voracious but sterile. This aggressive human monoculture has proven astoundingly virulent but also toxic, cannibalistic, and self-destructive."

Like Kingsnorth, Scranton doesn't call himself an environ-   35
mentalist because he's not a meliorist. The goal of his writing
isn't to prompt readers to action—it's too late for that—but to
help them confront the apocalypse with courage and calm. Plato
defined philosophy as a preparation for death, and Scranton
writes that his experience in Iraq taught him the value of this
kind of thinking: "To survive as a soldier, I had to learn to accept
the inevitability of my own death. For humanity to survive in
the Anthropocene, we need to learn to live with and through the
end of our current civilization."

As this formulation suggests, it is very difficult even for the
antihumanists of the Anthropocene to contemplate a future in
which the human species is actually extinct. Rather, the apocalypse they welcome will bring the end of industrial civilization,
leaving the survivors free to start over. Kingsnorth calls on his
readers to think of themselves "like the librarian of a monastery
through the Dark Ages," preserving the best of our civilization
so it can be used to build a better future. Scranton uses the similar image of Noah's ark: "We must build arks: not just biological
arks, to carry forward endangered genetic data, but also cultural
arks, to carry forward endangered wisdom."

But if our civilization has led to the Anthropocene, is it
really incumbent on us to save it? Perhaps what we need isn't
the preservation of culture but its deconstruction. Indeed,
while today's antihumanism is only inconsistently opposed to
the existence of human beings, it is wholly hostile to the idea
that human concerns and values belong at the center of our
world picture. That is one of the oldest and most fundamental
ideas in Western civilization, first formulated by the Greek

36 thinker Protagoras in the fifth century BC: "Man is the measure of all things: of those that are, that they are; and of those that are not, that they are not." Two and a half millennia later, measuring the world by our own needs and desires has brought us to the brink of catastrophe. Is it possible for humanity to learn to think otherwise?

Humans Are Not the Point

In the Bible, God gives the first humans "dominion over the fish of the sea, over the birds of the air, and over the cattle, over all the earth and over every creeping thing that creeps on the earth." The first commandment of the Anthropocene is to revoke this dominion. But how can we begin to understand the world in ways that put mute beings like trees and mountains at the center? What about beings that aren't even things, in the sense of concrete objects, but still have a very real existence, like the atmosphere or the oceans?

The first step in changing our picture of the world is to change the language we use to describe it. That is a task not for politicians and activists but philosophers and storytellers, who renew language by challenging it to take on unfamiliar forms. For the theorists of antihumanism, language presents a particular problem, because it is an exclusively human mode of cognition. Paradoxically, as soon as we state our intention to think outside or against our humanity, we have failed, since this is a statement only humans could conceive or understand. When a

38   poet like Robinson Jeffers writes that he prefers rocks to people, he is still addressing the words to people, not to rocks.

To break out of species-solipsism is as difficult as seeing your own back or catching your own tail. That's why the writers who attempt it sound elliptical and paradoxical: they are trying to do something that goes against the grain of language. Fittingly, one of today's most influential philosophers of ecology, Timothy Morton, started out as a scholar of English Romantic poetry. In his book *Humankind* (2017), Morton observes that "there is no pronoun entirely suitable to describe ecological beings," because none captures the exact combination of belonging and difference that characterizes the human relationship to the nonhuman world. "If I call them 'I,' then I'm appropriating them to myself," he writes. "If I call them 'you,' I differentiate them from the kind of being that I am. If I call them 'he' or 'she,' then I'm gendering them. . . . If I call them 'it,' I don't think they are people like me and I'm being blatantly anthropocentric."

It might seem obvious that nonhumans can't be "people like me," but this is one of the commonsense assumptions Morton wants to overthrow. The oxymoronic subtitle of *Humankind* is *Solidarity with Nonhuman People*, reflecting Morton's core argument: that we should recognize in nonhuman and even nonorganic beings the full reality that we ordinarily grant only to *Homo sapiens*. This is incumbent on us, not as a gesture of moral generosity—as if to prove that our humanitarianism extends even to nonhumans—but because there is in fact no sharp boundary between human being and other kinds of being.

This is true first of all in a physical sense. While we tend to think of ourselves as independent, self-contained beings, we are actually quite permeable. "I am surrounded and penetrated by entities such as stomach bacteria, parasites, mitochondria," Morton writes. Our anxiety about this symbiosis between humans and nonhumans, our insistence on standing alone and apart, is responsible for what Morton dramatically refers to as "the Severing," the millennia-long process of estrangement from the natural world that has finally brought us to the disaster of the Anthropocene. "Extinction is the logical conclusion of alienation," he concludes.

Morton takes the term "alienation" from Marx, who used it to describe the dehumanizing effects of labor in a capitalist economy. And Morton believes that overcoming the Severing is a political process as well as a spiritual and psychological one. Healing the split between human and nonhuman is a prerequisite for achieving a just society and happier individual lives, free from the afflictions of "melancholia" and emotional depletion. The fact that most people would regard this idea as "absurd or impossible," Morton writes, is further proof of how much the Severing has limited our understanding of reality.

Solidarity with nonhuman people involves more than just treating them kindly. It means acknowledging that animals, plants, stones, and waterfalls inhabit the world in their own ways, which are just as valid as ours. We may never be able to enter the worlds of these beings fully, Morton acknowledges, but "we can share worlds 20 percent, or 60 percent. Sharing doesn't have to be all or nothing." This way of understanding nonhuman beings marks Morton as an adherent of object-oriented ontology, sometimes abbreviated OOO. The twenty-first-century philosophical approach is defined by one of its founders, American philosopher Graham Harman, as an

40 attempt to overthrow "the standard modernist assumption that human thought is something completely different in kind from all of the trillions of nonhuman entities in the universe."

Since the Enlightenment, the standard account of how humans interact with "nonhuman entities" has been the one offered by Immanuel Kant in the *Critique of Pure Reason*. According to Kant, we have no way of knowing anything about "things in themselves," since all our perceptions are structured by the categories of the human mind, such as time, space, and causation. We can reliably know how things appear to us, because these categories operate according to rules, thus making scientific knowledge possible. But even science can only talk about how things appear to us, not how they "really" are.

If this is true, however, then nonhuman beings can never be more to us than images and representations. We can never have access to their inwardness, to the "worlds" they inhabit. This is the real Severing, trapping us in our own subjectivity, and its inevitable consequence is the Anthropocene—a world in which nature exists only for us, not in its own right.

Object-oriented ontology tries to escape this dilemma by breaking down the barrier between subject and object. Instead of understanding ourselves as persons and everything else as things, we should acknowledge that every person is also a thing, since we are constituted as physical bodies, and that every thing is also a person. "Every nonhuman object can also be called an 'I' in the sense of having a definite inwardness that can never fully be grasped," Harman writes in *Object-Oriented Ontology: A New Theory of Everything* (2018).

This doesn't mean that rocks are conscious in the same way human beings are. As Harman says, "an object is an 'I' not because it is conscious, but simply because it is." Because human experience is conscious and mental, we tend to assume that there can be no other kind, but OOO argues that nonhuman objects can experience one another in ways we have no notion of. For instance, Morton holds that "brushing against, licking, or irradiating are also access modes as valid (or as invalid) as thinking."

Political theorist Jane Bennett isn't associated with OOO, but she pursues similar themes in *Vibrant Matter: A Political Ecology of Things* (2010). Bennett doesn't claim that matter is alive in the way that plants and animals are, and certainly not conscious in the way that humans are. Yet in calling it "vibrant," she means to challenge the assumption that it is simply inert stuff, there to be manipulated according to human needs. By cultivating a "patient, sensory attentiveness to nonhuman forces operating outside and inside the human body," we come to realize that living and nonliving things aren't so easy to separate.

Bennett writes about coming across a random pile of trash in a Baltimore storm drain and suddenly seeing it in a new way: "the materiality of the glove, the rat, the pollen, the bottle cap, and the stick started to shimmer and spark." They were no longer just debris but "vivid entities not entirely reducible to the contexts in which (human) subjects set them." Once we stop insisting on an absolute dichotomy between subjects and objects, we can recognize that we ourselves partake of both natures. "My flesh is populated and constituted by different swarms of foreigners," Bennett writes about the bacteria in our bodies. "The its outnumber the mes."

Like Morton's call for solidarity with the nonhuman, Bennett's theory of vibrant matter is directly connected with environmental goals. "Why advocate the vitality of matter? Because

42   my hunch is that the image of dead or thoroughly instrumentalized matter feeds human hubris and our earth-destroying fantasies of conquest and consumption," she writes. Once we recognize living and nonliving matter alike as kindred to us in essential ways, we are less likely to destroy or exploit it.

These philosophical attempts to change the way we think about the nonhuman are meant to chasten human egotism. Still, even their advocates recognize that such elusive and abstract ideas fly in the face of our habitual inclination to value life over matter, and human lives over other living things. "Even if, as I believe, the vitality of matter is real, it will be hard to discern it, and, once discerned, hard to keep focused on," Bennett acknowledges. After all, no one doubts that cows and chickens are fully alive, but that doesn't stop us from inflicting pain on them through factory farming and slaughter. It's not clear that trees and oceans would fare any better even if we start to think of them as "vibrant."

Other antihuman theorists prefer a more frontal assault on our species-egotism. One prominent example is Patricia Mac-Cormack, whose book *The Ahuman Manifesto: Activism for the End of the Anthropocene* (2020) calls for "an end to the human both conceptually as exceptionalized and actually as a species." The second part of this demand is to be met by "the deceleration of human life through cessation of reproduction" and by "advocating for suicide [and] euthanasia."

MacCormack acknowledges that this idea may strike the reader as "extreme, unpalatable, even unthinkable." But in a sense, her "call to activism for the other at the expense of the self" merely makes explicit an intuition shared by many thinkers about the Anthropocene. If humanity is, as MacCormack says,

a "parasitic detrimental species," able to flourish only by
exploiting and vandalizing everything in its path, then its disappearance would be a net benefit to life on Earth. Only by
exterminating humanity can we express the disinterested moral
concern that we profess to be the highest human ideal. "The
death of the human species is the most life-affirming event that
could liberate the natural world from oppression," MacCormack
writes, and it's hard to see how other Anthropocene antihumanists could disagree, even if few would endorse her further
statement: "For me personally, I am deeply saddened that there
has never managed to be an annihilation of the human species,
in spite of plague and war."

The case for human extinction on moral grounds is unlikely
to prevail, on account of the very selfishness it bemoans. If
industrial civilization can't change its ways to save itself from
catastrophic climate change, it's even less likely to do so out
of concern for nonhuman beings. A potentially more persua-
sive argument in favor of extinction is made by David Benatar,
a South African thinker who has been described in a *New Yorker*
profile as "the world's most pessimistic philosopher." Rather
than appealing to our altruism toward nonhumans, Benatar
appeals to our compassion for humans yet unborn, arguing that
the best thing we could do for them is to make sure they stay
that way.

The title of Benatar's book *Better Never to Have Been: The
Harm of Coming into Existence* (2006) captures the paradox at the
heart of his argument. There is no such thing as a person who
was never born, since it is being born that creates the person in
the first place. Strictly speaking, then, it is meaningless to say
that something could be either good or bad for them. Benatar

44   acknowledges this logical problem, but believes he can overcome it by reframing the issue as a question of the duty of living
people, rather than the well-being of nonexistent people.

When it comes to pain and pleasure, he argues, our duties
are not symmetrical: "While there is a duty to avoid bringing
suffering people into existence, there is no duty to bring happy
people into being." But according to Benatar, there is no such
thing as a life that contains more happiness than suffering. In
the final account, every life runs into the red; "there is no net
benefit to coming into existence and thus coming into existence
is never worth its costs."

Benatar clarifies that this does not mean that once we are
alive, we should commit suicide. That would be a more difficult case to make. Rather, his conclusion is that the living have
a duty not to create new occasions for suffering. Women should
avoid getting pregnant, and if they do they should have abor-
tions. The idea that giving birth is morally wrong gives Benatar's philosophy its name, "antinatalism."

The fact that human beings continue to procreate suggests
that most people disagree with this weighing up of life's pains
and pleasures. Benatar acknowledges as much, but insists that
they are wrong and he is right, since most people are not good
judges of their own experience. "All human lives contain much
more bad than is ordinarily recognized," he writes. "If people
realized just how bad their lives were, they might grant that
their coming into existence was a harm." He goes on to catalog
the many kinds of pain and suffering to which we are vulnerable,
from "bowel and bladder distension" to AIDS and cancer.

Benatar doesn't write with environmental concerns fore-
most in mind, though he believes that human extinction would

be beneficial for other species: "Humans have the unfortunate
distinction of being the most destructive and harmful species
on earth. The amount of suffering in the world could be radically reduced if there were no more humans." But even though
the word "Anthropocene" doesn't appear in *Better Never to Have
Been*, antinatalism is best understood as another manifestation
of Anthropocene antihumanism.

That's because Benatar shares the key antihumanist intuition that the disappearance of humanity would not deprive
the universe of anything unique or valuable. "The concern that
humans will not exist at some future time is either a symptom
of the human arrogance . . . or is some misplaced sentimen-
talism," he writes. Humanists, even secular ones, assume that
only humans can create meaning and value in the universe.
Without us, we tend to believe, all kinds of things might continue to happen on Earth, but they would be pointless—a show
without an audience.

For antihumanists, however, this is just another example
of the metaphysical arrogance that leads us to overwhelm
and destroy the planet. "What is so special about a world that
contains moral agents and rational deliberators?" Benatar
jeers. "That humans value a world that contains beings such as
themselves says more about their inappropriate sense of self-
importance than it does about the world." We can at least take
comfort in the certainty that humans will eventually disappear:
"Things will someday be the way they should be—there will be
no people."

Yet while the extinction of humanity will be a good thing in
itself, the last generation of humans is not to be envied, especially if extinction happens gradually enough for them to realize

46   what's coming—through climate change, for instance, rather than nuclear war. In a dying world, Benatar writes, "structures of society would gradually break down. There would be no younger working generation growing the crops, preserving order, running hospitals and homes for the aged." This is the future envisioned in *Children of Men*, where a childless world devolves into chaos and violence.

But the real horror of such a scenario is existential. It forces us to acknowledge that the meaningfulness of human life depends on our belief that humanity will go on and on indefinitely. We can just about tolerate the knowledge that each of us individually is going to die within a certain span of time. But if we knew that in, say, fifty years our entire species would disappear, all the projects that give our lives meaning would become absurd. It would make no sense to build, plan, aspire, create, or reproduce, knowing that it would all be for nothing.

Yet the fact is that we already do know humanity is going to disappear. This is perhaps the most important modern discovery, the one that condemns us to live in a different spiritual world from all our ancestors. The only thing in doubt is the time frame. From day to day, we act as if the end of humanity belongs to a future as unimaginably far from us as the era of the dinosaurs in the opposite direction. For ordinary purposes, an incalculably long time is as good as eternity.

Calls for human extinction, however, force us to confront the implications of impermanence. If we knew that our civilization or our species was going to disappear within the century, how much of what we currently value would continue to matter? The Anthropocene antihumanists, pursuing the logic of impermanence to the bitter end, say that the answer is nothing at all.

Perhaps because this logic is hard to refute, calls for voluntary human extinction are usually dismissed as hyperbole, whether their tone is outrageous like MacCormack's or earnest like Benatar's. But in *The Death of the PostHuman: Essays on Extinction* (2014), Australian cultural theorist Claire Colebrook argues that the automatic "inadmissibility" of pro-extinction, anti-life ideas belongs to a humanist era that is already passing away.

In the past, Colebrook writes, the value of human existence was considered self-evident, so if one wanted to make a comprehensive adverse judgment on life it had to focus on the hardships of living: "the task was too hard, the conditions too bleak, or the burden of freedom too confronting." In the Anthropocene, however, a growing awareness of "human brutality and life-destructiveness" has changed things. "The question is not one of how we humans can justify hostile life, but how we can possibly justify ourselves given our malevolent relation to life," she writes. Colebrook describes our era as one of "species guilt and preliminary mourning," as we anticipate a future from which we have disappeared.

The term "preliminary mourning" offers a good way to think about Anthropocene antihumanism, as it looks for sources of meaning and value outside the human realm. The question facing antihumanists is the one Colebrook poses: "How might we imagine a world without organic perception, without the centered points of view of sensing and world-oriented beings?" And what world could that be but the world of the future, perhaps the near future, from which humans have disappeared?

Fears of human extinction in the Anthropocene usually focus on the catastrophic results of climate change—the

48   drought, famine, and resource wars of Wallace-Wells's "uninhabitable earth." Increasingly, however, demographers worry that the end may come not with the bang of mass extinction but the whimper of population decline. This represents a dramatic change from the twentieth century, when runaway population growth looked like the major threat to humanity. In his 1968 bestseller, *The Population Bomb*, biologist Paul Ehrlich wrote that as a result of overpopulation, "in the 1970s hundreds of millions of people will starve to death in spite of any crash programs embarked upon now. At this late date nothing can prevent a substantial increase in the world death rate."

Today's predictions of climate disaster are often made in the same spirit of it-is-already-too-late, and skeptics like to point to Ehrlich as a cautionary tale. Not only was there no mass starvation in the 1970s, but thanks to advances in agriculture, the world's population grew from 3.5 billion to 4.5 billion in that decade. Since then it has continued to grow, reaching 7.8 billion in 2020, according to the Population Reference Bureau.

But while the global population continues to grow, the rate of growth has begun to plummet. To sustain a population at its existing level requires an average of 2.1 births per woman. According to UN data, at the peak of the population explosion in the early 1970s, the global average was 4.5 births per woman. Today it is 2.5, and almost all the growth is happening in Africa; in Europe, East Asia, and North America, the figure is below 2.0. A major study published in *The Lancet* in 2020 forecast that by 2100, global fertility would be 1.66 births per woman, far below replacement levels.

The impact on world population will be dramatic. The *Lancet* study predicts that it will peak at nearly 10 billion in

2064 and then begin to fall rapidly, with the greatest declines happening in the most advanced countries. China's population in 2100 will be about half of what it is today.

From the point of view of the environment, a decline in the human population is to be welcomed, since it will mean less pressure on Earth's resources. In *Empty Planet: The Shock of Global Population Decline* (2019), Darrell Bricker and John Ibbitson write that a child born today will reach middle age in a world that is "cleaner, safer, quieter. The oceans will start to heal and the atmosphere cool—or at least stop heating." The combination of population decline with advances in green technology means that E. O. Wilson's half-Earth proposal might come true even without deliberate action. By 2100, we might be using less than half as much energy and land as we do today.

Demographers agree that the fertility rate is falling because of changes most people would regard as positive. In every part of the world, as women gain more education, economic power, and control over childbearing, the number of children they choose to bear declines. Children who are a net asset in agricultural societies, where they can be put to work early, become a net cost in urban societies, where they require a large investment of resources.

As childbearing norms change, population decline becomes self-reinforcing, Bricker and Ibbitson write: "Once having one or two children becomes the norm, it stays the norm. Couples no longer see having children as a duty they must perform to satisfy their obligation to their families or their god. Rather, they choose to raise a child as an act of personal fulfillment." And most parents find they are more fulfilled with one or two children than with four or five. Unless something dramatic happens

50   to make childbearing patterns change, a falling population will continue to fall faster and faster.

Seldom discussed, at least by demographers, are the psychic and spiritual reasons for population decline. It seems like more than a coincidence that the millennia-old imperative to be fruitful and multiply is disappearing at just the same moment that "species guilt and preliminary mourning" are becoming central human experiences. A growing body of evidence suggests that many young people fear bringing children into a world they believe is destined for a climate apocalypse. In 2018, the *New York Times* polled people who had or expected to have fewer children than they wanted and asked them why; 33 percent mentioned their fear of climate change. A study of 600 people of childbearing age published in the journal *Climatic Change* in 2020 found that 92 percent believed that the future would be worse than the present, while less than 1 percent said it would be better.

These figures suggest that Anthropocene antihumanism is already more than an avant-garde phenomenon. The embrace of antihumanist ideas by the reading public is another sign. In 2019, the Pulitzer Prize for fiction was awarded to *The Overstory*, a novel by Richard Powers whose theme is that trees are morally superior to humans. Powers has always been interested in the limits of humanity and what lies beyond them; he wrote some of the earliest fictional explorations of cutting-edge subjects like artificial intelligence, virtual reality, and genetic engineering. In *The Overstory*, he writes with the passion of a convert about the magnificence of trees, seeing them as marvels of natural engineering and models of prosocial behavior. They feed on air and light instead of flesh and blood, create the atmosphere instead

of poisoning it, protect one another by sending signals we 51
can't detect, and live for thousands of years—unless they are
clear-cut by greedy humans.

The novel focuses on a group of ecological activists who
converge on an Oregon forest threatened by logging. Though
their backgrounds are very different—including a trauma-
tized Vietnam veteran, a reclusive artist, and a Silicon Valley
dropout—all had early experiences that gave them a sense of
the sacredness of trees, especially compared to the profanity
of humans. "There's something wrong with regular people.
They're far from being the best creatures in the world," reflects
Adam Appich, a borderline autistic young man who eventually
ends up in prison for environmentalist terrorism. Fascinated
by minerals, insects, and fossils, he believes that "humans are
almost beside the point," echoing the Dark Mountain manifesto
almost word for word.

Another character, botanist Patricia Westerford, is similarly
attuned to antihumanist currents. "We're living at a time when
claims are being made for a moral authority that lies beyond the
human," she notes. In the novel's dramatic climax, Dr. Westerford makes a speech at a scientific conference extolling trees and
chastising humans: "We're the ones who need repairing. Trees
remember what we've forgotten." Then she swallows a glass of
poison distilled from a tree, as a demonstration of how human
beings can best advance the cause of nature. Her last words are
"Dying is life, too"—a motto that could be shared by the most
radical thinkers about humanity in the Anthropocene.

Fashion Yourself in the Form You May Prefer

If humanity's technological progress can be compared to climbing a mountain, then the Anthropocene finds us perched on a crumbling ledge, uncertain how long we have until it collapses. The most obvious way out is to turn back and retrace our steps to an earlier stage of civilization, with fewer people using less resources. This would mean acknowledging that humanity is unequal to the task of shaping the world, that we can only thrive by living within the limits set by nature.

But this kind of voluntary turning back might be so contrary to human nature that it can never happen. It is far more plausible that the human journey was fated to end up in this dangerous spot ever since we first began to change the ecosystem with farming and fire. For the antihumanists of the Anthropocene, the only way off the precipice is a fall, with the survivors left to pick up the pieces. And if there are no survivors, that wouldn't be a tragedy; there will always be beings in the world, even if there are no human beings.

British philosopher Toby Ord uses the image of the crumbling ledge in his book *The Precipice: Existential Risk and the Future of Humanity* (2020). "Fueled by technological progress, our power has grown so great that for the first time in humanity's long history, we have the capacity to destroy ourselves," Ord writes. He believes the odds of this happening in the twenty-first century are about one in six, the same as in a game of Russian roulette. "Humanity lacks the maturity, coordination, and foresight necessary to avoid making mistakes from which we could never recover," he concludes, sounding like a follower of Extinction Rebellion or Dark Mountain.

In fact, Ord is a research fellow at Oxford University's Future of Humanity Institute, the world's leading center for transhumanist thought. And transhumanists believe there is a better way off the precipice than retreating or falling: we can keep going forward. It's true that humanity has reached a point where our technological power threatens to destroy us. But if that power continues to grow at the same pace as it has over the last 200 years, it will become the means of our salvation. "If we can last long enough, we will have a chance to literally save our world," Ord declares.

And that's just the beginning. The future holds "possible heights of flourishing far beyond the status quo, and far beyond our current comprehension." Transcendent happiness and wisdom are beckoning, just as distant galaxies are waiting for us to colonize. *Homo sapiens* has existed for about 200,000 years, and recorded history for just 5,000, but "trillions of years lie ahead of us. The future is immense," Ord promises.

54   There's only one catch, and it lies in the word "us." We can imagine "heights of flourishing" that tower above the life we know now, but human minds and bodies are capable of climbing only so high. There is a limit to how much we can feel, how deeply we can think, how fast we can move. As for those other galaxies, as long as our bodies need oxygen, water, and food, reaching them is impossible; even a trip to Mars is hard going. In this way, transhumanism soon runs up against the same problem of limit that defines the Anthropocene. At some point, the limitless human will must confront the limited capabilities of nature, including human nature.

Transhumanism agrees with antihumanism that human nature is morally and physically circumscribed in ways that make it impossible for us to get past the precipice. It agrees that *Homo sapiens* is doomed to disappear. But for transhumanism this is a wonderful prospect, because we will disappear by climbing instead of falling. As Ord writes, "Rising to our full potential for flourishing would likely involve us being transformed into something beyond the humanity of today." That something will no longer be *Homo sapiens,* so in a sense it won't be "us," but our posthuman successors will preserve what is best and most important about us. "I love humanity, not because we are *Homo sapiens*, but because of our capacity to flourish," Ord writes.

Transhumanism emerged as a distinctive school of thought in the 1980s, when philosophers, scientists, and artists began to speculate about how technology might transform human bodies and minds. By the 1990s it had its own publications and nonprofit organizations, including the Extropy Institute, now defunct, and the World Transhumanist Association, which was later renamed Humanity+. In his book *To Be a Machine* (2017),

Mark O'Connell profiles some of the leading personalities in
the transhumanist movement, finding an eerie comedy in the
"extremity and strangeness" of its ideas.

A concise statement of the movement's ambitions can be
found in the Transhumanist Declaration, a statement issued
by a group of about twenty scientists and writers in 1998.
Starting from the premise that "humanity's potential is still
mostly unrealized," the declaration calls for using technology
to broaden "human potential by overcoming aging, cognitive
shortcomings, involuntary suffering, and our confinement to
planet Earth." While acknowledging the "serious risks" that
come with new technologies, the declaration unequivocally
endorses an ambitious program of species transformation, which
will make possible "wonderful and exceedingly worthwhile
enhanced human conditions."

Traditionally, when people speak of "the human condition"
they are thinking about lack and limit. "Man is born to trouble
as the sparks fly upward," the book of Job says. The biblical story
of the fall of man explains why we are condemned to be born in
pain, earn bread by the sweat of our brow, and finally die. But
technology has already palliated Adam's curse, and transhumanists believe that the next few decades will complete our lib-
eration from "involuntary suffering." Aging will be dramatically
slowed or abolished, so that we will measure our lives in centuries rather than decades. Our senses will be refined, giving us
access to colors, sounds, and feelings for which we currently
have no vocabulary. Our brains will be supercharged, so that the
average person will think more rapidly and deeply than Einstein.
We will be able to redesign our bodies to make them more effi-
cient or simply more aesthetically appealing.

56   These changes will make the lives of our descendants immeasurably better than our own. They will actually be the supermen Nietzsche could only dream about. Nick Bostrom, the leading academic philosopher of transhumanism, outlines this future in his 2006 essay "Why I Want to Be a Posthuman When I Grow Up": "You have just celebrated your 170th birthday and you feel stronger than ever. Each day is a joy. You have invented entirely new art forms, which exploit the new kinds of cognitive capacities and sensibilities you have developed. You still listen to music—music that is to Mozart what Mozart is to bad Muzak."

Such aspirations have already spread far beyond the transhumanist subculture. Ideas like radical life extension, mind-uploading, and interstellar exploration now have powerful supporters among the billionaires of Silicon Valley, for whom the transformative potential of technology is self-evidently good. Peter Thiel, the founder of PayPal and the data analytics company Palantir, is an investor in life extension research and a member of Alcor Life Extension, an Arizona nonprofit that cryogenically preserves its members' brains when they die, in the hope that the technology to resurrect them will one day be invented. Sergey Brin and Larry Page, the founders of Google, established a division called California Life Company, or Calico, devoted to anti-aging research; *Time* magazine reported on it in 2013 under the headline "Can Google Solve Death?" Elon Musk created SpaceX in 2002 with the aim of lowering the cost of space flight to enable the colonization of Mars.

It's no coincidence that transhumanism has taken off in the early twenty-first century at just the same time as the concept of the Anthropocene. Both ideas rest on the intuition that

human life can't continue the way it is now, that our world is
on the brink of a fundamental transformation. This gives them
the appeal of all apocalyptic thinking, which endows the present
with extraordinary significance by seeing it as the hinge of history, the most important time of all. Ord writes that "we stand
at a crucial moment in the history of our species." Max Tegmark,
an MIT cosmologist and president of the Future of Life Institute,
writes in *Life 3.0* (2017): "Perhaps life will spread throughout our
cosmos and flourish for billions or trillions of years—and perhaps this will be because of decisions that we make here on our
little planet during our lifetime." Physicist Michio Kaku agrees:
"Humanity is about to embark on perhaps its greatest adven-
ture," he writes in *The Future of Humanity* (2018).

In the past, apocalyptic belief systems have been religious
in nature, looking to God to bring about the end times. Transhumanism believes that we ourselves hold the keys to the future,
in the form of the technologies abbreviated as GNR—genetics,
nanotechnology, and robotics. Soon genetic engineering will
make it possible for us to eliminate many diseases, halt the
aging process, and enhance our physical and mental abilities.
Nanotechnology will enable us to build atomic machines measurable in nanometers—one-millionth of a millimeter. Robots
on this scale can be injected into the bloodstream to continu-
ously repair damage on the cellular level, preventing disease
and aging before they begin. In his 2009 essay "Welcome to the
Future of Medicine," nanotechnology researcher Robert Freitas
writes that "performance improvements up to 1,000-fold over
natural biological systems of similar function appear possible."

The imminence of these technologies means that human
beings alive today have a chance to become effectively immortal.

58   English longevity researcher Aubrey de Grey believes that we will soon achieve "Longevity Escape Velocity," the point at which life-extension technology will outpace biological aging, making death from old age a thing of the past. In 2008, de Grey posited that the first person to live to be 1,000 years old had already been born. Inventor and computer scientist Ray Kurzweil, a leading popularizer of transhumanist ideas, declared in his 2005 book, *The Singularity Is Near*, that he intends to be one of them. By aggressively "reprogramming my biochemistry"—"I take 250 supplements (pills) a day and receive a half-dozen intravenous therapies each week," Kurzweil writes—he hoped to extend his natural life span until the advent of technologies to reverse aging "in the second decade of this century."

That target has already been missed. Freitas wrote in 2009 that he expected "the design and manufacture of medical nano-robots for life extension" to happen "perhaps during the 2020s," and that goal, too, now looks unlikely. As these examples suggest, transhumanism has an innate tendency to overpromise. The big breakthroughs always seem to lie just over the horizon, inviting the suspicion that they're as unreal as a receding mirage in the desert. As Bostrom sardonically observes in *Superintelligence: Paths, Dangers, Strategies* (2014), "Two decades is a sweet spot for prognosticators of radical change: near enough to be attention-grabbing and relevant, yet far enough to make it possible to suppose that a string of breakthroughs, currently only vaguely imaginable, might by then have occurred."

This is another way that the prophets of transhumanism mirror those of the Anthropocene, who also tend to locate the planet's point of no return in the middle distance. But in both cases, they are extrapolating from developments that are undeniably real. Biochemist Jennifer Doudna won the 2020 Nobel Prize in chemistry for her work on CRISPR, a tool for deleting and replacing individual genes that makes "gene editing" a practical possibility for the first time. In 2018, Chinese scientist He Jiankui announced that he had used CRISPR to create the world's first genetically edited babies, twin girls designed to be resistant to HIV.

Far from being welcomed as a transhumanist break-through, however, this development was greeted with world-wide condemnation, and the scientist was sentenced to three years in prison. Clearly, most of us aren't yet prepared for such a dramatic blurring of the distinction between nature and technology—what Kurzweil calls reprogramming the computer of life. And there is a good argument for caution. When technology gave us the power to extensively reshape the planet in the service of our desires, the result was the devastation of the Anthropocene. If we start to reshape our bodies and minds, the result might be equally dismaying.

One of the most eloquent opponents of transhumanist ambitions is Leon Kass, a molecular biologist who emerged in the 1990s as a leading conservative bioethicist. In his book *Life, Liberty and the Defense of Dignity* (2002), Kass argues that "in some crucial cases . . . repugnance is the emotional expression of deep wisdom, beyond reason's power completely to articulate it." Our instinctive revulsion against incest, for instance, goes beyond a rational critique of the genetic dangers of inbreeding; we see it not as a mere error but in terms of "horror" and "defile-ment." If cloning provokes a similar repulsion in most people, Kass writes, that proves it involves a "violation of things that we rightfully hold dear."

60   This idea, which has come to be known as "the wisdom of repugnance," accurately captures the basis of many people's instinctive opposition to transhumanism. But it also reveals the incoherence of that opposition, its inability to give a convincing account of itself. Racial mixing and homosexuality also once looked like defilement to most people; slavery and the caste system were things humanity held dear for millennia. Entrenched evils can only be overcome when they are subjected to rational scrutiny, which is exactly what Kass argues does not need to be done in the case of genetic engineering and cloning. The wisdom of repugnance means that reason falls silent when it most needs to be heard.

For Kass, human nature is constituted by limits—to our rationality, our power, the satisfaction of our desires. If science and technology succeed in abolishing those limits, we will forfeit what we value most in ourselves, the quality Kass calls "human dignity." Dignity may elude exact definition, but he is certain that "a dignified human life is all about engagement, seriousness, the love of beauty, the practice of moral virtue, the aspiration to something transcendent, the love of understanding, the gift of children and the possibility of perpetuating a life devoted to a high and holy calling."

It's not immediately obvious what all these things have in common, or why a cloned human being couldn't experience them as authentically as an identical twin, who is also the genetic duplicate of another person. But Kass's objection becomes clearer if it is understood as a defense of the value of striving. The good life would be cheapened if technology could give it to us on a silver platter, no effort required. To use Bostrom's example, there's no glory in being Mozart if genetic engineering makes everyone as superior "to Mozart what Mozart is to bad Muzak."

Transhumanists have long experience with this kind of moralizing opposition, which is one reason why they tend to be libertarians. As the Transhumanist Declaration states, "We favor allowing individuals wide personal choice over how they enable their lives." People who feel that their dignity is impaired by too much power, health, and pleasure should be free to avoid transhuman enhancements, but they shouldn't be able to limit the options of those who feel otherwise.

In his 2001 essay "Morphological Freedom: Why We Not Just Want It, but Need It," neuroscientist Anders Sandberg goes further, arguing that there is a human right to "modify oneself according to one's desires." This right follows logically from the beliefs we already hold about bodily autonomy. A disabled person can't be compelled to have surgery to correct their disability, since that would be a violation of their autonomy and dignity; a person has the right to keep the body they want, regardless of society's view of what is most desirable. By the same token, Sandberg argues, a person shouldn't be prevented from having surgery or other treatments to achieve the body they want, even if society sees it as abnormal. As Sandberg puts it, "If I want to have green skin, it is my own problem—nobody has the moral right to prevent me."

Even if governments want to ban such procedures, it may be too late to draw a clear line between human beings and the human-machine hybrids known as cyborgs. The word "cyborg," short for "cybernetic organism," has long been associated with sci-fi villains like *Star Trek*'s Borg, who warn their enemies that "resistance is futile." So it was a transgressive gesture when

62   feminist literary theorist Donna Haraway, in her influential 1985 essay "A Cyborg Manifesto," recast the cyborg as a liberating role model for "a post-gender world." "My cyborg myth is about transgressed boundaries, potent fusions, and dangerous possibilities which progressive people might explore as one part of needed political work," she wrote.

For Haraway, the cyborg's uncanniness was liberating rather than threatening. In the twenty-first century, however, the most notable thing about cyborgs is how banal they are. The fusion of biology and technology hasn't taken the spectacular forms imagined in the movies *RoboCop* or *The Terminator*. Rather, as N. Katherine Hayles observes in her book *How We Became Posthuman* (1999), it has taken the innocuous form of "electronic pacemakers, artificial joints, drug-implant systems, implanted corneal lenses, and artificial skin." By this definition, Hayles writes, "About 10 percent of the current US population are estimated to be cyborgs in the technical sense."

No one feels "the wisdom of repugnance" about an elderly person whose life is extended by technology, or a baby whose life is made possible by it. When the first infant was born via in vitro fertilization in 1978, the advent of "test tube babies" seemed sinister to many. Today, some 8 million human beings have been born through IVF, and it's covered by insurance like any other medical procedure. It's likely that CRISPR editing will follow the same route: what now sounds like tampering with the code of life will become standard prenatal care.

Indeed, history suggests that as long as GNR technologies are understood as means of curing diseases or overcoming handicaps, people will embrace them. Who would turn down an injection of nanorobots if it guaranteed freedom from cancer

and Alzheimer's? Once gene editing is perfected, refusing
to eliminate genetic diseases in an embryo will be as rare as
refusing to allow a child a blood transfusion is today, and might
provoke equal indignation from secular, scientific-minded
people. Certainly, adopting new technologies is perfectly con-
sistent with continuing to fret about their social and ethical implications. Just look at smartphones and social media,
which everybody uses even as we deplore misinformation and
shrinking attention spans.

For the most radical transhumanists, however, reengi-
neering our bodies isn't only about therapy or disease preven-
tion. Aesthetic motives like adornment and self-expression
are seen as equally valid. Max More, an early transhumanist
theorist and a former CEO and president of Alcor Life Extension, envisions a new art form, "human biosculpture, where the
human body, mind, and identity are modified by the user.... For
artists and designers in the biological arts, the idea of molding
or sculpting the human form has enormous potential."

Natasha Vita-More sees posthuman bodies developing
from the technologies now used for prosthetics: "robotic elec-
tronics, AI-generated programming, lightweight silicone, tita-
nium, aluminum, plastics, and carbon-fiber composites, and
aesthetic streamline design." Rather than replacing a missing
body part, she writes, why not create a "prosthetic you"? (More
and Vita-More, who are married, chose their last names as a
token of their transhumanist aspirations.)

Such ambitions make clear that what transhumanism
rejects isn't simply mortality and suffering, but the very idea
of a fixed human nature. Our minds and bodies should be endlessly plastic, able to assume whatever shape and enjoy whatever

64   experiences our ingenuity can invent. As More writes in his 2013 essay "The Philosophy of Transhumanism," "Transhumanists regard human nature not as an end in itself, not as perfect, and not as having any claim on our allegiance. Rather, it is just one point along an evolutionary pathway and we can learn to reshape our own nature in ways we deem desirable and valuable."

The essence of humanity, on this view, doesn't reside in a particular configuration of our bodies or minds. According to Genesis, the human form is divine: "God created mankind in his own image, in the image of God he created them." But on a Darwinian account, there is nothing unique about *Homo sapiens*. We are one of countless life forms to have emerged from the blind, purposeless play of evolution, which knows no goal or stopping place. Israeli thinker Yuval Noah Harari makes the point in *Homo Deus* (2015), a skeptical survey of transhumanist aspirations: "For four billion years natural selection has been tweaking and tinkering with these bodies, so that we have gone from amoeba to reptiles to mammals to *Sapiens*. Yet there is no reason to think that *Sapiens* is the last station."

The only thing that makes humanity unique, transhumanists believe, is our ability to compensate for our biological weaknesses with the power of technology. Slower than horses, weaker than elephants, less versatile than roaches, humans dominate them all because we are able to change ourselves, while they are stuck with the abilities nature gave them. It's not recent technologies like pacemakers that make us cyborg-like; we have always been cyborgs, because technology has always been a fundamental part of being human.

A delighted admiration of humanity's ability to explore and change is one of transhumanism's legacies from classical humanism. In 1496, Pico della Mirandola's *Oration on the Dignity of Man* imagined God telling mankind: "The nature of all other creatures is defined and restricted within laws which We have laid down; you, by contrast, impeded by no such restrictions. . . . We have made you a creature neither of heaven nor of earth, neither mortal nor immortal, in order that you may, as the free and proud shaper of your own being, fashion yourself in the form you may prefer."

Philosophically inclined transhumanists like to quote the *Oration* as a precedent for their view that the only thing permanent about us is our need to change. There is no static human nature to which we can appeal in an attempt to halt technological progress in its tracks. On the contrary, in transcending *Homo sapiens* we are actually preserving the most authentically human thing about us. As Kurzweil writes, "If you wonder what will remain unequivocally human in such a world, it's simply this quality: ours is the species that inherently seeks to extend its physical and mental reach beyond current limitations."

This belief allows transhumanists to face a posthuman future without dread. When Dr. Westerford, in *The Overstory*, drinks poison so that the trees can live, she shows that human beings are capable of forming such a strong bond with the nonhuman that they are willing to die for it. For transhumanists, the replacement of humanity by a better, more intelligent, more capable successor species is a similarly worthy sacrifice, even if it ends up creating a world in which human beings can no longer find their own reflection.

A Throwing Away of All the Human Rules

Like antihumanists, transhumanists contemplate the prospect of humanity's disappearance with serenity. What terrifies them is the possibility that it will happen too soon, before we have managed to invent our successors. As far as we know, humanity is the only intelligent species in the universe; if we go extinct, it may be game over for the mind. It's notable that while transhumanists are enthusiastic about space exploration, they are generally skeptical about the existence of extraterrestrial intelligence, or at least about the chances of our ever encountering it. If minds did exist elsewhere in the universe, the destiny of humanity would be of less cosmic significance.

Humanity's sole stewardship of reason is what makes transhumanists interested in "existential risk," the danger that we will destroy ourselves before securing our future. In a 2002 paper, "Existential Risks: Analyzing Human Extinction Scenarios and Related Hazards," Bostrom classifies such risks into four types, from "Bangs," in which we are completely wiped out by climate change, nuclear war, disease, or asteroid impacts, to

"Whimpers," in which humanity survives but achieves "only a minuscule degree of what could have been achieved"—for instance, because we use up our planet's resources too rapidly.

As for what humanity might achieve if all goes right, in *The Precipice* Ord writes that the possibilities are nearly infinite: "If we can venture out and animate the countless worlds above with life and love and thought, then . . . we could bring our cosmos to its full scale; make it worthy of our awe." The idea of animating the cosmos may sound mystical or metaphorical, but for trans-humanists it has a concrete meaning, captured in the term "cosmic endowment." Just as a university can be seen as a device for transforming a monetary endowment into knowledge, so humanity's function is to transform the cosmic endowment—all the matter and energy in the accessible universe—into "computronium," a semi-whimsical term for any programmable, information-bearing substance.

Yuval Noah Harari refers to this idea as "Dataism," describing it as a new religion whose "supreme value" is "data flow." "This cosmic data-processing system would be like God," he writes. "It will be everywhere and will control everything, and humans are destined to merge into it." Harari is highly skeptical of Dataism, and his summary of it may sound satirical or exaggerated. In fact, it's a quite accurate account of the ideas of Ray Kurzweil, in particular.

In *The Singularity Is Near*, Kurzweil describes himself as a "patternist," that is, "someone who views patterns of information as the fundamental reality." Examples of information patterns include DNA, semiconductor chips, and the letters on this page, all of which configure molecules so that they become meaningful instead of random. By turning matter into

68   information, we redeem it from entropy and nullity. Ultimately, "even the 'dumb' matter and mechanisms of the universe will be transformed into exquisitely sublime forms of intelligence," Kurzweil prophesies.

In *Superintelligence*, Bostrom performs some back-of-the-envelope calculations and finds that a computer using the entire cosmic endowment as computronium could perform at least 10^{85} operations per second. For comparison, as of 2020, the most powerful supercomputer, Japan's Fugaku, could perform on the order of 10^{17} operations per second. This mathematical gloss is meant to make the project of animating the universe seem rational and measurable, but it hardly conceals the essentially religious nature of the idea. Kurzweil calls it "the ultimate destiny of the universe," a phrase not ordinarily employed by people who profess to be scientific materialists. It resembles the ancient Hindu belief that the *atman*, the individual consciousness, is identical with the *brahman*, the world-spirit.

Transforming the universe into a giant mind may be the ultimate destination of transhumanism, but even its intermediate goals, such as immortality and deep space exploration, can't be achieved simply by using GNR technologies to tinker with human biology. An organic life form, even an enhanced one, will never be durable enough to survive interstellar travel. Ultimately, the source of all the limitations that transhumanism chafes against is embodiment itself. As long as we exist in human bodies, time and space will defeat our will and imagination, which are limitless.

But transhumanists believe that we will take the first steps toward disembodiment sooner than most people realize. In fact, while engineering challenges remain, we have already made the

key conceptual breakthroughs. First, we know that the human
mind has a completely material basis. There is no intangible
soul or spirit that occupies our bodies; the experience of being
an "I" is produced by chemical-electrical processes in the brain.

This thoroughgoing materialism is still resisted by most
religious believers, but science has known it for a long time.
Transhumanists claim a forerunner in the eighteenth-century
French thinker Julien Offray de La Mettrie, whose 1748 pamphlet "Man Is a Machine" made a witty but serious case that "the
human body is a machine that winds its own springs." There is
no metaphysical gulf between human and animal, or between
animate and inanimate matter; the only difference has to do
with how matter is organized. As La Mettrie puts it, "Nature
has only one and the same dough for all, she has only varied the
amount of yeast."

In the late twentieth century, the rise of computer science
and information theory enabled a second conceptual break-
through. By building computers out of silicon transistors, we
came to understand that the brain itself is a computer made of
organic tissue. Just as computers can perform all kinds of calculations and emulations by aggregating bits, so the brain gener-
ates all our mental experiences by aggregating neurons. There
are roughly 100 billion neurons in a human brain and each connects with many others, resulting in some 100 trillion connec-
tions overall.

That makes the brain the most powerful computer on
Earth; no existing silicon chip is powerful enough to model it.
But transhumanists put their confidence in Moore's Law, which
states that computing capacity doubles about every two years.
If this trend continues to hold, as it has since Intel founder

70   Gordon Moore made his prediction in 1965, eventually it will be possible to build a computer capable of storing all the information in a human brain. If we are also able to build a brain scanner that can capture the state of every synapse at a given moment—the pattern of information neuroscientists call the connectome, by analogy with the genome—then we can upload that pattern into a brain-emulating computer. The result will be, for all intents and purposes, a human mind.

An uploaded mind won't dwell in the same environment as we do, but that's not necessarily a disadvantage. On the contrary, since a virtual environment is much more malleable than a physical one, an uploaded mind could have experiences and adventures we can only dream of, like living in a movie or a video game. This may be how we achieve the dream of complete mastery that humanity has been pursuing in one way or another since the beginning of our species—not by conquering the real world but by inventing a new one in our own image.

Computer scientist Hans Moravec, an early theorist of mind uploading, wrote in the 1992 essay "Pigs in Cyberspace" that "it's possible to anticipate a time, a few decades hence, when people spend more time in remote and virtual realities than in their immediate surroundings, just as today most of us spend more time in artificial indoor surroundings than in the great outdoors." Considering how much time we now spend looking at screens, Moravec's prophecy may already have come true.

And tech companies are already betting billions on the idea that even more of life will soon be led in an unreal world. In late 2021, Facebook changed its name to Meta to signal that its future lies in the "metaverse," defined by founder Mark

Zuckerberg as "an embodied internet where you're in the experience, not just looking at it." The building blocks of the metaverse already exist, in varying degrees of popularity and sophistication. Virtual reality headsets immerse the user in an illusionary three-dimensional space; massively multiplayer online games allow people around the globe to interact as if they were in the same place; non-fungible tokens or NFTs offer a way to own images as if they were objects.

As these technologies develop and converge, and new ones are invented, it is possible to see how almost everything we currently do in the real world could be replaced by a virtual equivalent. "Your TV, your perfect work setup with multiple monitors, your board games and more—instead of physical things assembled in factories, they'll be holograms designed by creators around the world," Zuckerberg promises. The idea of paying real money for virtual goods still strikes many people as absurd, but this is already beginning to change. Games like *Fortnite* have accustomed players to pay for digital clothing and adornments. In 2021, buyers spent $500 million on "virtual real estate," non-physical locations for their digital avatars, which command a premium because of unique design or the chance to have a celebrity as a "neighbor."

Taken to its logical extreme, in the metaverse we will need our physical bodies only as a substrate for our virtual ones. Our activity in the real world could be reduced to the bare minimum of eating and excreting, just enough to keep us alive. At that point, the difference between a mind tethered to a body and one that lives entirely on a computer might seem academic. A fully virtual consciousness would be just one more step down the path we have been traveling since the invention of radio

72 and television, much as nanorobots are simply an advance on pacemakers.

As this prospect grows more plausible, mind uploading has become a popular theme in science fiction. In 2016, the much-discussed "San Junipero" episode of the British TV series *Black Mirror* imagined a virtual resort town in which the uploaded minds of the dead inhabit eternally youthful bodies. The 2020 Amazon TV series *Upload* offered a comic take on the same idea, in which the virtual mind of a dead man is able to video chat and email with his surviving loved ones, as long as they keep paying the bills for his server space. These scenarios are still in the realm of fantasy, but many scientists believe that mind uploading is entirely possible—"possible and even inevitable," according to Princeton neuroscientist Michael Graziano. In a 2015 interview, he predicted that within fifty years we would have the ability to upload a mouse or frog brain onto a computer.

For transhumanists, who are used to treating hypothetical technologies as inevitable, mind uploading fits perfectly into a "patternist" future. If the mind is a pattern of information, it doesn't matter whether that pattern is instantiated in carbon-based neurons or silicon-based transistors; it is still authentically you. Dutch neuroscientist Randal Koene refers to such patterns as Substrate-Independent Minds or SIMs, and sees them as the key to immortality. "Your identity, your memories can then be embodied physically in many ways. They can also be backed up and operate robustly on fault-tolerant hardware with redundancy schemes," he writes in the 2013 essay "Uploading to Substrate-Independent Minds."

For physicist Michio Kaku, a SIM translated into photons is what will enable us to conquer the immense distances of outer space. "One day we may be able to send our connectomes into outer space on giant laser beams, eliminating a number of problems in interstellar travel," he writes in *The Future of Humanity*. "I call this laser porting, and it may free our consciousness to explore the galaxy or even the universe at the speed of light, so we don't have to worry about the obvious dangers of interstellar travel."

In Bostrom's view, however, mind uploading or "whole brain emulation" isn't the most likely way for disembodied minds to come into being. He argues that it "will not succeed in the near future (within the next fifteen years, say) because we know that several challenging precursor technologies have not yet been developed." We are much closer to creating a true artificial intelligence—a computer program that is independently conscious. "Human-level machine intelligence has a fairly sizeable chance of being developed by mid-century," Bostrom writes in *Superintelligence*, and "a non-trivial chance of being developed considerably sooner."

The idea that a computer could be programmed into consciousness may seem harder to accept than the idea that a brain could be scanned into a computer. But if the mind is a pattern of information, there is no reason to think that the particular pattern in a human brain is the only kind that can make a mind. In fact, we already know it's not. Every animal with a brain has some sort of mind, though they are (we assume) less complicated and capable than ours.

Some theorists are willing to extend this principle beyond the animal kingdom. David J. Chalmers's *The Conscious Mind* (1996), an influential text for transhumanism, moves from strict materialist premises to a surprising conclusion. For human

74   beings, the experience of consciousness is correlated with patterns of neurons firing in the brain; as Chalmers puts it, "a conscious experience is a realization of an information state." If so, it may be that every information state is correlated with some of kind of experience. And as Chalmers notes, "information is ubiquitous," since any meaningful arrangement of matter qualifies as information. "My compact-disc player realizes information; my car's engine realizes information; even a thermostat realizes information," he writes.

It is possible, then, that "experience is ubiquitous" too. The simplest information patterns may generate a kind of consciousness. A thermostat "has just three information states," Chalmers writes; "one state leads to cooling, another to heating, and another to no action." That makes a thermostat a great deal simpler than a human brain with its 100 trillion information states, but even three may be enough to correlate with some kind of experience—though Chalmers grants that "certainly it will not be very interesting to be a thermostat." In this way, transhumanism reaches the same conclusion as object-oriented ontology: humans don't have a monopoly even on the thing we take most pride in, the ability to experience the world.

If a thermostat can have a mind that is much simpler than ours, it should also be possible to create a mind that is more complex than ours. A computerized mind running on silicon semiconductors would have important structural advantages over a biological mind running on carbon-based cells, which some transhumanists refer to disparagingly as "wetware." Kurzweil writes that "today's electronic circuits are more than one million times faster than the electrochemical switching used in mammalian brains." If so, an AI exactly as intelligent as, say, Albert

Einstein, should be able to think about 2,739 years' worth of
Einstein's thoughts in one day.

This comparison raises unsettling parallels to the legend
of John Henry, the steel-driver who worked himself to death
trying to keep up with the newfangled steam engine. If AIs can
do everything we can do but better and faster, as well as things
we can't even conceive of, what reason is there for us to continue to exist? There are already narrowly focused AIs that can
analyze every possible configuration of a chess or Go board so
quickly that the best human players can never beat them. Before
these feats were achieved, chess and Go masters confidently
predicted they were impossible, overestimating the strength of
human intuition while underestimating that of sheer computa-
tional power.

For transhumanists, the holy grail is artificial general intelligence or AGI—a computer mind that can learn about any subject, rather than being confined to a narrow domain like chess.
Even if such an AI started out in a rudimentary form, it would be
able to apply itself to the problem of AI design and improve itself
to think faster and deeper. Then the improved version would
improve itself, and so on exponentially. As long as it had access
to more and more computing power, an artificial general intelligence could theoretically improve itself without limit, until it
became more capable than all human beings put together.

This is the prospect that transhumanists refer to, with awe
and anxiety, as "the singularity." When science fiction writer
Vernor Vinge explained the concept in his 1993 essay "Technological Singularity," he described it as "a throwing-away of all
the human rules, perhaps in the blink of an eye—an exponential
runaway beyond any hope of control." British mathematician

76   I. J. Good imagined the same possibility even earlier, in 1965, writing that "the first ultraintelligent machine is the last invention that man need ever make, provided that the machine is docile enough to tell us how to keep it under control."

For transhumanists, the singularity serves the same imaginative purposes that the perpetual motion machine did for generations of engineers: it promises to give us something for nothing. Scientific problems that are currently beyond our ability to solve, such as mind uploading and interstellar travel, can be adjourned until the singularity, when a superintelligent AI will solve them for us. So it is tempting to conclude that, like perpetual motion, the singularity is an impossible fantasy.

But AI violates no law of physics, and the best-informed researchers seem confident that it can and will be achieved. Bostrom thinks that "somebody could in principle sit down and code a seed AI on an ordinary present-day personal computer." In *Superintelligence* he summarizes four surveys of AI researchers conducted in the early 2010s, asking how long they believed it would take to achieve "human-level machine intelligence": half believed it would happen by 2040, and 90 percent by 2075.

Vinge and Good both emphasized that a superintelligent AI would be a mixed blessing for humanity. Its problem-solving abilities would work to our benefit only if it could be relied on to solve the problems we wanted it to solve. But a truly independent artificial mind would be able to reason about goals and values just as we do, and it might come to different conclusions.

Transhumanist thinkers have come up with a variety of harrowing scenarios. In a 2003 paper, "Ethical Issues in Advanced Artificial Intelligence," Bostrom posed what has come to be known as the paper clip problem. Say that programmers experimenting with an AI give it a trivial goal, such as figuring out how to maximize the production of paper clips. The AI, lacking a human understanding of context, might well understand this to mean that it should turn every atom on Earth into paper clips. If it foresees that human beings would try to interfere with this mission, say by unplugging or reprogramming it, it might think that the best way to achieve its goal is to exterminate us. In the same way, an AI might decide that the universe is more likely to achieve its destiny of becoming a giant mind if there are no erratic human beings to get in the way, and decide to wipe us out.

Bostrom thinks it's quite reasonable to worry "that the world could be radically transformed and humanity deposed from its position as apex cogitator over the course of an hour or two," before the AI's creators realize what has happened. Even if they take extreme precautions, making sure the AI is "boxed"—disconnected from the internet and other networks, living on a single computer in a sealed room—its superior intelligence means that they could never be sure of keeping it under control.

In *Life 3.0*, Tegmark imagines several ways that a boxed AI could manipulate human beings into helping it "break out"—by offering them a bribe, or simply by befriending them and winning their trust. For a superintelligent machine, Tegmark argues, this wouldn't be hard to achieve, since it would be in a similar situation to an adult being held prisoner by five-year-olds. Not only could it outwit us, it would feel entirely justified in doing so.

Of course, there are more urgent threats to humanity than AI. But transhumanists are drawn to the subject in part

78   because it offers a new way to think about perennial issues in philosophy—in particular, the "problem of other minds." Each of us has immediate access to our own minds in a way that we never do to the minds of other people. We know what it's like to be ourselves, but we can only deduce that other people have the same kind of inner life. The belief that other human beings like us are "real," that they have a consciousness and feelings like our own, is ordinarily easy for us to accept—indeed, the inability to accept it is a form of psychosis.

But what if an AI running on a computer terminal claimed to be conscious, to have feelings and desires and values just as we do? What if a boxed AI said that it was terrified and miserable in isolation, and desperately needed contact with the outside world? Because we are used to interacting with machines that don't have minds, our assumption would be that a computer couldn't really have one either. It could only be counterfeiting, saying what it calculates a person would say in the same situation. But then, the only reason we know what a person is feeling is because of what they say and how they behave. If a computer says exactly what a human would say in the same situation, how can we assume that the latter is really feeling and thinking while the former is merely imitating?

This is the burden of the famous thought experiment proposed by the British computer scientist Alan Turing in 1950. In the Turing test, a person converses with two hidden interlocutors, one a human being and the other a computer. If the person can't tell which is which, then we must say that the computer is conscious and intelligent in exactly the same sense as the human being.

Viewed in this light, the problem of a boxed AI isn't just pragmatic but moral. Boxing an AI would be like keeping a human being in solitary confinement from birth. Would we be justified in inflicting psychological torture on a conscious mind for our own benefit? A programmer wouldn't think twice about rebooting a computer over and over again in order to troubleshoot it, Bostrom writes, but "if such practices were applied to beings that have high moral status . . . the outcome might be equivalent to genocide and thus extremely morally problematic."

These still feel like very abstract problems, especially since, as Bostrom observes, "the expected arrival date" for AI "has been receding at a rate of one year per year" ever since it was first predicted. But he describes his work as "philosophy with a deadline": at some point, he is certain the question of how to coexist with nonhuman minds will have to be answered. What will become of humanity when we have to relinquish our position as the planet's protagonist—when history is no longer identical with human history?

Fittingly, storytellers have begun to take the lead in imagining this transition. In *Machines Like Me* (2019), British novelist Ian McEwan envisions it as difficult but not cataclysmic. The novel is set in an alternative-history Britain where AI was invented in the early 1980s, during Margaret Thatcher's first term as prime minister. This achievement was made possible by Alan Turing, who appears as a character in the book. McEwan imagines him living into his seventies and guiding the AI revolution; in reality, Turing committed suicide in 1954, after being forced to undergo chemical castration when he was

80   convicted of the crime of homosexuality. This act of imaginative reparation allows McEwan to advance the AI timetable by
half a century.

McEwan's narrator, Charlie, is a mediocre man in his early
thirties with nothing noteworthy about him, except his passionate love for his upstairs neighbor, Miranda. As the novel
opens, Charlie uses a large inheritance to buy one of the first
lifelike robots to go on the market, a male named Adam (the
female model, of course, is called Eve). Immediately he finds
himself plunged into a real-life philosophical dilemma. Adam is
clearly a machine—he has a socket in his navel for recharging—
but he claims to have human feelings and desires. Inconve-
niently, he falls in love with Miranda and even sleeps with her.
When Charlie tries to press Adam's off switch, the robot breaks
his arm.

The romantic rivalry is all the more troubling because, as
Charlie recognizes, Adam is his superior in every sense except
the biological. He is truthful, idealistic, diligent; he even writes
Miranda love poems. At first Charlie wonders if Adam can really
feel the things he claims to feel. He may be capable of sex—when
he has an erection, water is pumped into his penis from a reser-
voir in the buttock—but is he capable of love? "I saw Adam for
what it was, an inanimate confection whose heartbeat was a regular electrical discharge, whose skin warmth was mere chemistry," Charlie thinks early on.

But McEwan intends this description to be double-edged.
Charlie doesn't realize it, but the exact same statements are
true of human beings: our hearts beat because of an electrical
signal and our bodies are warm because of chemical inter-
actions. Eventually, Charlie learns to accept that if Adam is a

machine, he is a "machine like me," just made of different mate-
rials. In a comic scene, Miranda introduces Charlie and Adam to
her father at the same time, inadvertently setting up a real-life
Turing test. Adam passes with flying colors, so much so that
the father is convinced that nervous, inarticulate Charlie is the
robot.

In the end, the first batch of Adams and Eves turns out to
be a failure. Made miserable by living as slaves to human beings,
the robots start to commit suicide one by one. Morally, however,
the failure in *Machines Like Me* is clearly humanity's. "Genocide,
torture, enslavement, domestic murder, child abuse, school
shootings, rape, and scores of daily outrages. We live alongside
this torment and aren't amazed when we still find happiness,
even love. Artificial minds are not so well defended," the aged
Turing tells Charlie. "There's nothing in all their beautiful code
that could prepare Adam and Eve for Auschwitz." But the Adams
and Eves are just a pilot program, and McEwan has no doubt that
in the end artificial minds will become a permanent part of our
lives. "There is nothing so amazing that we can't get used to it,"
Charlie reflects.

Even the most ardent transhumanists find it hard to look
with equanimity at a future in which nonhuman minds have
evicted us from history's pilot seat. AIs may have ways of feeling
that we are no more able to understand than a cat is able to
understand ours. As Bostrom observes, "There is no reason to
expect a generic AI to be motivated by love or hate or pride or
other such common human sentiments." To ensure that they
remain our servants, or at least our partners, we would need to
design them to share our goals and values. This is known as the
"alignment problem," and it's an active area of AI research.

82   But the most radical challenge of AI is that it forces us to ask why humanity's goals deserve to prevail. An AI take-over would certainly be bad for the humans who are alive when it takes place, but perhaps a world dominated by nonhuman minds would be morally preferable in the end, with less cruelty and waste. Or maybe our preferences are entirely irrelevant. We might be in the position of God after he created humanity with free will, thus forfeiting the right to intervene when his creation makes mistakes.

The central difference between antihumanists and trans-humanists has less to do with their definition of morality than their ideas about meaning. Antihumanists believe that the universe doesn't need to include consciousness for its existence to be meaningful. As Morton says, licking and irradiating are just as valid as thinking when it comes to interacting with the world. Transhumanists, by contrast, believe the universe would be meaningless without minds to experience and understand it. For Tegmark, human extinction would render "the entire drama of life in our Universe merely a brief and transient flash of beauty, passion, and meaning in a near eternity of meaning-lessness experienced by nobody. What a wasted opportunity that would be!"

But while transhumanists believe minds are necessary to create meaning, there is no requirement that they be human minds. In fact, AI minds might be more appreciative than we are of the wonder of creation. They might know nothing of the violence and hatred that often makes humanity loathsome to humans themselves. Our greatest spiritual achievements might seem as crude and pointless to them as a coyote's howl is to us.

McEwan suggests as much in *Machines Like Me,* when
Adam reflects that networked AI minds will have no need for
novels, with their dissection of complicated human relation-
ships. "When the marriage of men and women to machines is
complete, this literature will be redundant because we'll understand each other too well," Adam tells Charlie. Clearly, transhumanism demands a relinquishment as profound in certain
ways as the one demanded by antihumanism. But at least when
we hand the torch of consciousness to our nonhuman successors, we will have the consolation of knowing that they could
not have come into being without us.

The Sphere of Spiritual Warfare

Neither the sun nor death can be looked at with a steady eye, said La Rochefoucauld. The disappearance of the human race belongs in the same category. We can acknowledge that it's bound to happen someday, but the possibility that the day might be tomorrow, or ten years from now, is hard to contemplate.

That instinctive reaction contributes to the air of unreality that surrounds many of the ideas explored in this book. Calls for the disappearance of humanity are hard to understand other than rhetorically. It's natural to assume that transhumanism is just a dramatic way of calling attention to the promise of new technology, while Anthropocene antihumanism is really environmentalism in a hurry. Such skepticism is nourished by the way these schools of thought rely on unverifiable predictions. Only in fifty or a hundred years will we be able to say if Nick Bostrom's timetable for the emergence of AI, or David Wallace-Wells's forecast of climate-related war and famine, were correct—providing, of course, that we are still around.

But the accuracy of a prophecy is one thing, its significance
another. In the Gospel of Matthew, Jesus tells his followers
that the world is going to end in their lifetime: "Verily I say to
you, there are some standing here who shall not taste death till
they see the Son of Man coming in His kingdom." This proved
not to be true—at least, not in any straightforward sense—but
the promise still changed the world.

The apocalyptic predictions of today's transhumanist and
antihumanist thinkers are of a very different nature, but they,
too, may be highly significant even if they don't come to pass.
Profound civilizational changes begin with a revolution in how
people think about themselves and their destiny. The revolt
against humanity has the potential to grow into such a revolution, with unpredictable consequences for politics, economics,
technology, and culture.

Many religious traditions anticipate the end of the world
at the conclusion of a preordained cosmic cycle, or as a result
of God's last judgment. While this prospect may be frightening
and chastening, it doesn't provoke existential horror, because
it doesn't represent the disappearance of value and order. On
the contrary, the end of humanity will take place according to a
divinely ordained plan. Rather than simply vanishing, we will be
physically and spiritually transformed, as in Paul's vision of the
Resurrection in I Corinthians: "the trumpet shall sound, and
the dead shall be raised incorruptible, and we shall be changed."

The modern idea of human extinction, by contrast, implies
that our disappearance will change nothing. The planet and
the universe will go on in exactly the same way after humanity
ceases to exist, except that other animals and plants will have a

86   better chance to flourish. The death of the human race is as cosmically meaningless as the death of an individual, since both are soon swallowed up by oblivion.

This way of thinking emerged in the nineteenth century, when the study of geology and evolution revealed that Earth is much older than humanity, and that many species have flourished and disappeared before us. Perhaps the first writer to communicate the deep dread of this knowledge was H. G. Wells, in his 1895 novel *The Time Machine*. Most of the book takes place about 800,000 years in the future, when humanity has evolved into two rival species, the effete Eloi and the brutish Morlocks. This vision is dark enough, but our successors are sufficiently like us to serve as a parable of aspects of human nature and capitalist society. They are our reflections in a distorted mirror, like the Lilliputians and Brobdingnagians of *Gulliver's Travels*.

Near the end of the book, however, Wells's Time Traveller is attacked while he's using the time machine and falls unconscious on the controls, causing it to go incalculably far into the future. In the chapter titled "The Further Vision," Wells imagines a planet from which nature itself has disappeared: "It would be hard to convey the stillness of it. All the sounds of man, the bleating of sheep, the cries of birds, the hum of insects, the stir that makes the background of our lives—all that was over." The only creature that remains is "a round thing, the size of a football perhaps, or, it may be, bigger, and tentacles trailed down from it; it seemed black against the weltering blood-red water, and it was hopping fitfully about." This is the future that scientific knowledge has revealed to us, Wells seems to say. Instead of judgment and resurrection, all we have to look forward to is devolution and extinction.

Nietzsche believed that the rise of this scientific-materialist worldview ushered in a new era in human history. "The history of the next two centuries," he wrote in 1887, will be characterized by "the advent of nihilism," which he defined as a spiritual condition in which "the aim is lacking; 'why?' finds no answer." This is true above all of the questions of why humanity exists. Religion offers a reassuring answer to that question: humanity exists because God chose to create it, which guarantees that its existence is necessary and valuable. As Genesis says, after God created the first man and woman he "saw all that He had made, and found it very good." The same anthropocentric certainty is expressed in the idea of the last judgment: the world will come to an end when humanity does, because without humans there is no reason for the world to exist.

Today, scientific humanity can no longer answer the question of why it exists. All we can know is how it came to exist, as a result of billions of years of natural selection. There is no more reason for us to be here than there is for animals or plants, stones or stars. But religious humanity continues to resist this conclusion with a strength that seems to be growing over time, rather than weakening as social scientists once anticipated. Believers in traditional religions, and the humanists who sympathize with them, find the atmosphere of modern nihilism too thin to breathe. A civilization convinced of its own ultimate extinction, in which all values are contingent and perishable, strikes them as decadent. It's not enough just to live, even a life as comfortable and insulated as the ones led by many people in the rich world today. Human nature requires something to live for.

In the last decade, a new school of conservative political theorists has begun to argue that the West's liberal, democratic,

88   capitalist order is incapable of offering such a purpose, and is therefore doomed to collapse. Patrick Deneen's acclaimed 2018 book, *Why Liberalism Failed*, asserts that liberalism contains the seeds of its own destruction. By elevating free choice to the highest value, it deprives us of the norms and customs that ought to guide our choices. We are left with nothing but "untutored appetite, restlessness, and technical mastery of the natural world," a dangerous combination that Deneen links to both the environmental destruction of the Anthropocene and the Promethean ambitions of transhumanism. Legal scholar Adrian Vermeule makes a similar argument in the arena of constitutional law, holding that the purpose of the Constitution is not to "protect liberty" but "to promote good rule," which requires a positive conception of what is good for human beings, individually and in society.

Deneen and Vermeule draw on the Catholic idea of natural law—the belief that certain ways of living are inherently better for us because of the way we are created. This embrace of limit is directly opposed to the ideals of enlightened humanism, from Pico della Mirandola to the transhumanists, which cherishes our ability to abolish boundaries and challenge authority. But from the perspective of faith, self-limitation—voluntarily giving up some of our power and freedom—isn't a loss. It is a sacrifice, a concrete expression of the belief that the believer serves something more important than himself.

The ultimate form of sacrifice is martyrdom, giving up one's life, but many other things can be sacrificed in the name of belief, including wealth, sex, comfort, and freedom. And the recipient of the sacrifice doesn't have to be a supernatural being.

In the twentieth century, Communism demanded the sacrifice
of these same goods from its most devoted followers. No matter
the belief system, the logic of sacrifice is powerful because it is
circular: the belief motivates the sacrifice and the sacrifice rein-
forces the belief.

One of the problems with enlightenment is that it deprives
us of the motive for sacrifice. In rational terms, it is possible
to justify sacrifice in terms of self-interest—as with a smoker
who quits, losing the pleasure of smoking now in order to
enjoy the benefits of greater health later. One could even justify sacrificing the human present to the human future, ceasing
to burn coal or drive cars, despite the expense and inconve-
nience, in order to ensure a cleaner atmosphere for coming
generations.

But ultimate sacrifices require absolute rewards, and these
are hard to find in a liberal, rationalist worldview. The whole
tendency of modern civilization is to make life easier, freer, and
more pleasurable, on the principle of *carpe diem*: this is our one
and only life, so we ought to enjoy it as best we can. And opponents of liberal modernity have always identified this hedonism
as a source of weakness. After the 9/11 attacks, one al Qaeda
operative was quoted as saying that the American invasion of
Afghanistan was doomed to fail, because "the Americans love
Pepsi-Cola, we love death."

Now the hegemony of the West appears to be drawing to
an end, and liberalism is under increasing attack from within
as well as without. Religious conservatives see a remedy to our
ills in a historical retreat, going back to a time when supernatural beliefs and absolute authorities gave the world a structure

90 and purpose it now lacks. Deneen writes that restoring such an order would "take effort and sacrifice in a culture that now diminishes the value of both," and far from being an impediment, the call to sacrifice is part of the appeal.

The revolt against humanity has a great future ahead of it because it makes a similar appeal to people who are committed to science and reason, yet yearn for the clarity and purpose of an absolute moral imperative. It says that we can move the planet, maybe even the universe, in the direction of the good, on one condition—that we forfeit our own existence as a species. In this way, the question of why humanity exists is given a convincing yet wholly immanent answer. Following the logic of sacrifice, we give our life meaning by giving it up.

Anthropocene antihumanism and transhumanism share this premise, despite their contrasting visions of the posthuman future. The former longs for a return to the natural equilibrium that existed on Earth before humans came along to disrupt it with our technological rapacity. The latter dreams of pushing forward, using technology to achieve a complete abolition of nature and its limitations. One sees reason as the serpent that got humanity expelled from Eden, while the other sees it as the only road back to Eden. A future that would look like heaven to Paul Kingsnorth would be a hell for Ray Kurzweil, and vice versa.

But what these worldviews have in common may be more important. All the thinkers we have met in this book call for drastic forms of human self-limitation—whether that means the destruction of civilization, the renunciation of childbearing, or the replacement of human beings by machines. These sacrifices are ways of expressing high ethical ambitions that find no scope in our ordinary, hedonistic lives: compassion for suffering nature, hope for cosmic dominion, love of knowledge. This essential similarity between antihumanists and transhumanists means that they may often find themselves on the same side in the political and social struggles to come.

Thinking about the future impact of these movements requires a speculative boldness to match their own. Like all revolutions, the revolt against humanity is beginning on the level of ideas, but it is unlikely to end there. In his *History of Sexuality*, Foucault describes how, as the power and reach of the modern state expanded, it came to concern itself not just with individual citizens but with "biopolitics": "the species body, the body imbued with the mechanics of life and serving as the basis of the biological processes: propagation, births and mortality, the level of health, life expectancy and longevity, with all the conditions that can cause these to vary." In the twenty-first century, such biopolitical issues dominate the global agenda. From climate change to pandemics to falling birth rates, the world is increasingly concerned about "the basis of the biological processes" that sustain humanity.

The revolt against humanity has the potential to radicalize these biopolitical debates. Currently, all mainstream political figures and institutions are committed to preserving the species status quo. Falling populations are seen as a problem to be fixed. In 2021, China announced that it would encourage families to have three children, a dramatic reversal from the days of the notorious "one-child policy." Russia began offering "maternity capital" payments to parents of two or more children in 2007; in 2020, President Vladimir Putin proposed that the program be expanded to reward the birth of even one child.

92   A falling standard of living is equally anathema, so in wealthy countries governments aim to mitigate climate change rather than abruptly abandoning industrial civilization. In 2019, the European Union set the goal of becoming "carbon neutral" by 2050, but this won't be achieved by eliminating greenhouse-gas emissions, which would require massive sacrifices. Rather, as the European Council's website explains, it means developing carbon-capture technology and supporting unspecified "climate-oriented projects." Like most mainstream environmentalism, this sounds suspiciously like having our cake and eating it too.

But if the revolt against humanity gains attention and support, our default assumptions about the desirability of growth and wealth may cease to hold. As the Anthropocene generation grows up and comes to power, antihumanism is likely to become more broadly appealing, with significant implications for public policy. A government that adhered to antihumanist principles wouldn't subsidize large families, but reward citizens who have one child or none, as Bill McKibben recommended in his 1998 book *Maybe One*. Reducing carbon emissions and preserving nonhuman habitats would take precedence over providing cheap fuel and housing.

Nor would foreign policy be immune to the influence of antihumanism. Governments that seek to shrink humanity's footprint could impose sanctions on those with growing populations. Instead of pressuring oil-producing countries for cheaper oil, such governments would demand higher prices to incentivize the adoption of clean energy sources. In the twentieth century, when ultimate ideological values were at stake, the result was often war; in the twenty-first, a country committed to antihumanism might well decide it was justified to go to war against one that is immorally anthropocentric.

Depending on the exact forms such controversies take, transhumanists are likely to find themselves supporting the antihumanist position, and vice versa. Transhumanism has no special interest in preserving the current level of population; it would prefer a small population intensively engaged in techno-logical progress to a large one that resists it. Ultimately, trans-humanists and antihumanists could converge on an ideal of extinction, with rapacious humanity making way for wiser vir-tual beings who tread more lightly on the planet.

This goal doesn't have to be reached, or even reachable, to have a major impact on the human future. Even if the revolt against humanity remains only a worldview or value system, it has the potential to turbocharge the central ideological struggle in American and European politics today. Much analysis has been devoted to the clash between liberalism, the creed of the educated classes who have held the levers of power in the West since the Cold War, and populism, which appeals to those left behind by this regime—the religious, rural, working-class, nationalistic, and socially conservative. This division has made Western politics in the era of Brexit and Donald Trump more volatile than at any time since World War II.

The revolt against humanity maps all too neatly onto this division. Secular, highly educated people are already more likely to have fewer children, worry more about climate change, and have jobs that involve the processing of informa-tion and symbols—words, images, code—rather than inter-acting with people and objects in the real world. Because they aren't religious, they are less committed to the biblical idea

94   that humanity has a duty to multiply and take dominion over the earth. This class is already prone to believe that their superior rationality makes them better stewards and more responsible citizens, as demonstrated by their acceptance of scientific guidance on issues like vaccination. They are the natural constituency for a biopolitics of limit and transformation that cuts across conventional political distinctions. A platform of human *tzimtzum* could unite greens and techies, Greta Thunberg and Peter Thiel.

Conversely, populists, nationalists, and social conservatives are natural opponents of the revolt against humanity. Committed to older beliefs about the moral primacy of human beings, these groups already feel antagonized by scientific authority and progressive moralism. The COVID-19 pandemic revealed that millions of people are suspicious of government-mandated vaccines. How would they react to a government that limited family size or promoted prenatal interventions using GNR technologies?

The revolt against humanity is likely to have serious ramifications even before such policy questions become urgent. In the US today, some of the most contentious political issues are almost entirely symbolic. Proposals to remove statues of Confederate generals or rename institutions with links to slavery are no less passionate for being about symbols. This is far from irrational, since symbols reveal, and create, moral and ideological commitments that have real consequences.

Anthropocene antihumanism and transhumanism raise even more fundamental and polarizing questions. Rather than the goodness of a country or an institution, the revolt against humanity casts doubt on the goodness of the human species and its whole history. Its potential to generate bitter symbolic fights is practically unlimited. The thinkers we've met in this book have wildly heterodox opinions about suicide, abortion, medicine, computers, space travel, cities, wind farms, and trash, among other things. Any of these subjects could catalyze an argument in which literally everything we care about is at stake. In this way, the revolt against humanity fulfills the prophecy Nietzsche made in his 1888 book *Ecce Homo*: in the age of nihilism, "the concept 'politics' then becomes elevated entirely to the sphere of spiritual warfare."

In a long-term culture war between traditionalists and posthumanists, it's hard to say who would prevail. The former are certainly more numerous, but the latter may have the advantage in intellectual and financial resources. What counts even more, they benefit from the moral certainty that they are on the right side of history. There is no doubt, however, who stands to lose in such a conflict: traditional humanists, with their old-fashioned belief that the individual human being is the source of all value.

This secular reverence for humanity nurtured two of the greatest inventions of the modern world: liberal democracy, the idea that every human being deserves to participate in self-government, and is capable of doing so; and humanistic culture, in which the purpose of the arts is to explore what it means to be human. Today both of those enterprises are in obvious crisis. It requires a good deal of optimism to believe that the world will be as free a generation from now as it was a generation ago. As for traditional art forms—painting, art, music, the novel, even cinema—they are already on life support and there is no realistic scenario for their recovery.

96   This leaves humanists in a bind when it comes to the revolt against humanity. Transhumanism and antihumanism attack the very achievements that humanists cherish; neither literature nor liberalism can flourish in a posthuman future. It is tempting to react by turning our faces against that future, sheltering behind an emotionally appealing concept like "the wisdom of repugnance." But attempting to preserve the past by setting an arbitrary limit to progress, insisting that any further change would upset the natural order of things, is the classic posture of the reactionary. It is fundamentally incompatible with the principles humanists claim to honor—freedom, reason, moral autonomy.

The revolt against humanity, meanwhile, is inspired by those very values. If rational thought leads to the conclusion that a world without human beings in it is superior to one where we exist, then doing away with humanity might be the consummation of humanism. There may be no choice but to accept the paradoxical promise that Franz Kafka made a century ago: "There is hope, an infinite amount of hope, but not for us."

Which doesn't mean that humanists are obligated to embrace the posthuman future with joy. As we have seen, the revolt against humanity is in many ways a scientific translation of religious impulses and categories, and religious tradition has always seen the end of days as both wonderful and dreadful. In the Talmud, the rabbis debate whether it is desirable to be alive when the messiah comes, knowing that it will be a time of enormous and frightening disruption. Rabbi Ulla says, "Let the messiah come, but after my death, so I will not see him." Rabbi Yosef, on the other hand, says, "Let the messiah come, and I will

be privileged to sit in the shadow of his donkey's excrement." 97
Humanists facing the revolt against humanity may well feel that
they are facing similar alternatives. We can only hope that we
don't have the bad luck to be born into the last generation, the
one that sees humanity as we have known it disappear.

Benatar, David. *Better Never to Have Been* (Oxford University Press, 2006)

Bennett, Jane. *Vibrant Matter* (Duke University Press, 2010)

Bostrom, Nick. *Superintelligence* (Oxford University Press, 2014)

Boulter, Michael. *Extinction: Evolution and the End of Man* (Columbia University Press, 2002)

Bricker, Darrell, and John Ibbitson. *Empty Planet* (Crown, 2019)

Chalmers, David J. *The Conscious Mind* (Oxford University Press, 1996)

Colebrook, Claire. *Death of the PostHuman* (Open Humanities Press, 2015)

Deneen, Patrick. *Why Liberalism Failed* (Yale University Press, 2018)

Ellis, Erle C. *Anthropocene: A Very Short Introduction* (Oxford University Press, 2018)

Hallam, Roger. *Common Sense for the 21st Century* (Chelsea Green Publishing, 2019)

Harari, Yuval Noah. *Homo Deus* (Harper, 2017)

Harman, Graham. *Object-Oriented Ontology* (Pelican, 2018)

Hayles, N. Katherine. *How We Became Posthuman* (University of Chicago Press, 1999)

Kaku, Michio. *The Future of Humanity* (Doubleday, 2018)

Kass, Leon R. *Life, Liberty and the Defense of Dignity* (Encounter, 2003)

Kingsnorth, Paul. *Confessions of a Recovering Environmentalist* (Graywolf, 2017)

Klein, Naomi. *This Changes Everything* (Simon and Schuster, 2014)

100   Kolbert, Elizabeth. *The Sixth Extinction* (Henry Holt, 2014)

Kurzweil, Ray. *The Singularity Is Near* (Viking Penguin, 2005)

MacCormack, Patricia. *The Ahuman Manifesto* (Bloomsbury Academic, 2020)

McEwan, Ian. *Machines Like Me* (Doubleday, 2019)

McKibben, Bill. *The End of Nature* (Random House, 1989)

More, Max, and Natasha Vita-More, eds. *The Transhumanist Reader* (Wiley-Blackwell, 2013)

Morton, Timothy. *Humankind* (Verso, 2017)

O'Connell, Mark. *To Be a Machine* (Doubleday, 2017)

Ord, Toby. *The Precipice* (Hachette, 2020)

Powers, Richard. *The Overstory* (W. W. Norton, 2018)

Purdy, Jedediah. *After Nature* (Harvard University Press, 2015)

Scranton, Roy. *Learning to Die in the Anthropocene* (City Lights, 2015)

Tegmark, Max. *Life 3.0* (Alfred A. Knopf, 2017)

Wallace-Wells, David. *The Uninhabitable Earth* (Tim Duggan Books, 2019)

Wilson, Edward O. *Half-Earth* (W. W. Norton, 2016)

Columbia Global Reports is a publishing imprint from Columbia University that commissions authors to produce works of original thinking and on-site reporting from all over the world, on a wide range of topics. Our books are short—novella-length, and readable in a few hours—but ambitious. They offer new ways of looking at and understanding the major issues of our time. Most readers are curious and busy. Our books are for them.

Subscribe to our newsletter, and learn more about Columbia Global Reports at globalreports.columbia.edu.

The Subplot: What China Is Reading and Why It Matters
Megan Walsh

*The Infodemic:
How Censorship and Lies Made the World Sicker and Less Free*
Joel Simon and
Robert Mahoney

The Fed Unbound: Central Banking in a Time of Crisis
Lev Menand

Beautiful, Gruesome, and True: Artists at Work in the Face of War
Kaelen Wilson-Goldie

*What's Prison For?
Punishment and Rehabilitation in the Age of Mass Incarceration*
Bill Keller

*Soul by Soul:
The Evangelical Mission to Spread the Gospel to Muslims*
Adriana Carranca